Collaboration and Networking in Education

Daniel Muijs · Mel Ainscow · Chris Chapman ·
Mel West

Collaboration and Networking in Education

Springer

Prof. Daniel Muijs
University of Southampton
School of Education
Highfield Campus
Southampton
United Kingdom
d.muijs@soton.ac.uk

Prof. Mel Ainscow
University of Manchester
School of Education
Oxford Road
M13 9PL Manchester
United Kingdom

Dr. Chris Chapman
University of Manchester
School of Education
Oxford Road
M13 9PL Manchester
United Kingdom

Prof. Mel West
University of Manchester
School of Education
Oxford Road
M13 9PL Manchester
United Kingdom

ISBN 978-94-007-0282-0 e-ISBN 978-94-007-0283-7
DOI 10.1007/978-94-007-0283-7
Springer Dordrecht Heidelberg London New York

Printed on acid-free paper

Springer is part of Springer Science+Business Media (www.springer.com)

Contents

Chapter 1
Introduction: Networking in Schools

1.1 Introduction

Traditionally, a network has been defined as a set of actors (individuals or organisations such as schools) connected by a set of ties, which can be of a more or less formal nature (Borgatti & Foster, 2003). The principle of networking and collaboration has become more prevalent and more widely studied in organisations both in the private and public sectors. This move is seen to arise from advances in the understanding of learning and especially the perceived advantages of collaborative learning, and, in the private sector at least, from an increased need for innovation stemming from intensified international competition, that is seen to necessitate flexible networks that can reduce the exposure of firms to risk and uncertainty (Cohen & Levintal, 1990; Borgatti & Foster, 2003). Arguably, this need for increased innovation is also present in the education system, as demands on the system have increased due to a greater political interest in education. This has resulted from both a perceived growth of the importance of education in the globalised knowledge economy which requires highly educated citizens, and a (perceived) diminution of the influence of politics on the economic sphere in the light of heightened global competition and a broad consensus, at least in the developed economies, around a free market approach to economic policy, leaving education as one of few major spheres which politicians see themselves as able to influence. The demands for ever higher levels of achievement, intolerance of failure and, in some countries at least, concern over the remaining inequities that characterise the system mean that schools too are set demanding goals requiring innovation. This is especially challenging for schools serving disadvantaged communities, that are required to show high levels of raw performance, while being able to directly affect at most 25% of the variance in pupil achievement, the remainder being down to pupil-level factors (Teddlie & Reynolds, 2000). Furthermore, while both national policies and school improvement programmes and initiatives can show evidence of impact, they have not been able to close the gap in achievement between high and low SES schools (West et al., 2006).

In part as a result of this, many educational systems have experimented with networking and collaborative approaches to improvement. For example, in the 1990s

D. Muijs et al., *Collaboration and Networking in Education*,
DOI 10.1007/978-94-007-0283-7_1,

over 100 schools were involved with the National Schools Network in Australia. In the US, there are a number of school improvement networks including the League of Professional Schools and the Coalition of Essential Schools. The school improvement network, Improving the Quality of Education for All (IQEA) exists in diverse contexts ranging from Hong Kong to Iceland. However, it would seem it is the English context where the commitment to networking and collaboration has been greatest. During the past decade significant resources have been invested in collaborative arrangements including Education Action Zones (EAZ), Excellence in Cities (EiC), Leadership Incentive Grant (LIG), Schools facing Extremely Challenging Circumstances (SfECC), Network Learning Communities (NLCs), and various Specialist Schools partnership and network programmes. These developments have been aimed at relocating innovation closer to schools in order to generate greater collective capacity for change and have relied on teachers working together across organisational boundaries without any significant structural changes to their organisations.

1.2 The Impact of Networking and Collaboration in Education

Interestingly, in light of the interest of both policy and practice in networking and collaboration in education, more research appears to focus on the conditions under which networks and collaborative arrangements between schools can be effective than on whether they have a positive impact in the first place. Most studies are cross-sectional in nature, though some longitudinal work exists, usually focussing on a 2–3 year period. The overall evidence of the impact of networking and collaboration on school effectiveness and improvement is therefore limited, though there is some evidence from individual programmes, such as the SSAP run by the Specialist Schools Trust which partnered low achieving schools 'lead' schools that supported them and showed positive outcomes for schools in the study (Chapman & Allen, 2005).

OECD (2000) findings suggest creating collaborative structures around schools is more likely to result in deeper organisational learning both collectively and individually. This work shows that school networks are locations in which specialised knowledge can be created and transferred within collaborative contexts. Senge (1990) emphasises collaborative learning and team skills as being the key to successful and sustainable organisational development rather than individual skills and individual learning. His work suggests that networks of schools do not just facilitate innovation but the evidence would suggest that they offer the possibility of new ways of working. It has been shown that they offer the potential for redesigning local systems and structures by promoting different forms of collaboration, linkages, and multi-functional partnerships (Senge et al., 2000). Consequently, school networks are increasingly being seen as a means of facilitating innovation and change as well as contributing to large-scale reform (Chapman & Fullan, 2007; Ainscow & West, 2006; Hargreaves, A., 2003a; OECD, 2000).

In 2005 the Centre for the Use of Research and Evidence in Education (CUREE) published a review of the impact of networking arrangements of various kinds on students, teachers, schools, and their communities. The review locates studies that claim impact on student attainment and engagement, on teachers on schools, and on parents.

With regard to pupil attainment, studies by Montgomery (2001) and Greenberg (1996) are cited as evidence of high impact. Bielefeldt et al. (1999) also offer evidence of increases in student skills and progression. Further, the Montgomery and Bielefeldt studies claim significant impact on levels of student engagement, with supporting evidence from studies by Adler (1995) and Thurlow et al. (1999). Though findings from these studies are robust, it should be understood that these were, for the most part, closely focussed studies, targeted on particular student groups, rather than on whole school communities. Nevertheless, CUREE also reports a number of studies claiming some impact to support these cases (e.g. Reyes & Phillips, 2002; Riley & Jordan, 2004). While the review also finds some studies (e.g. Sanders, 1999) that focussed on the impact of networking on practitioners, ignoring any student effects, and others reporting no impact (e.g. Pinon, Samii-Shore, & Batchelder, 2002), overall, the balance of evidence seems to be that collaborative arrangements *can* impact on students, though not all do.

The review cites 11 studies that have reported changes in teachers knowledge and skills as a result of network 'interventions', the majority of which 'led to clearly identifiable behaviour changes' (CUREE, 2005). Six of these (Bielefeldt et al., 1999; Adler, 1995; Gettinger et al., 1999; Greenberg, 1996; Thurlow, 1999) were considered to offer evidence of high impact judged by such criteria as observable changes in classroom behaviour, changes in attitudes towards parental involvement, improved classroom management and deepened knowledge, and understanding of teaching and learning. Again, there were some less promising studies: Kahne et al. (2001) reported high levels of teacher mistrust, and reluctance to commit to externally determined goals, and Pinon et al. (2002) noted that school principals seemed to be more stirred by collaborative work than were their teachers, but these are comments on the way collaboration has been practised, rather than collaboration per se. In fact, we have made similar observations ourselves in the early phase of collaborative activity, when the 'groundrules' and operating principles have not been adequately clarified. However, this has not necessarily proved a barrier to the development of cohesive collaborative cultures.

The review's comments on school level impact are disappointing. It seems they were unable to locate anything that had any substantial contribution to make to understanding the ways collaborative arrangements influence school structures and processes. But, there are impacts on the school community reported, which themselves imply that something different is going on within schools. The main areas of community development identified are increased involvement of parents in the life of the school and closer links with local communities. Tantalisingly, there is little comment on how such networking arrangements influence either governance arrangements, or relationships with the responsible education authority or district personnel.

Looking close to home, in England, Chapman and Harris (2004), reviewing the impact of *Network Learning Groups* on schools facing challenging circumstances offer a number of propositions. These suggested that successful collaboration hinged on the use of key levers within the network. Levers include a clear focus on teaching and learning, which encourages teachers to focus on and experiment with their own classroom practice; distributed leadership, which draws in the various members of the schools in the network and allocates real tasks to them; a shared commitment to professional development at all levels, including headship, and the capacity to identify and to exploit opportunities for external support. This last point is especially interesting, as it implies that far from joining together in order to establish a common boundary, successful networks remain open to their environments and the opportunities to draw on resources to be found there.

With regard to impact, the authors are measured. They point to important structural and cultural changes that have taken place within schools in the networks. They are able to identify clear advances in school performance in some instances. But they suggest that if the networks are to become a significant improvement strategy for all the schools involved, then they will need also to become rather more rigorous arrangements too. They voice particular reservations about the suitability of current NLGs as improvement vehicles for schools facing challenging circumstances, pointing out that in planning collaborative arrangements for such schools internal capacity (Stoll, 1999), internal structures and practices (Potter, Reynolds, & Chapman, 2002) and particular external factors (Muijs, Harris, Chapman, Stoll, & Russ, 2004) would all need to be taken into consideration.

Chapman and Allen (2005), in a report for the *Specialist Schools Trust,* concluded that targeted, collaborative approaches to support the development of a specialised school system were proving highly effective. At its simplest, the partnerships had demonstrated greater increases in student achievement over their lifetime than the national average increase, and also increased or maintained added value scores. At a broader level of analysis, there seemed to have been improvements in school climate, staff morale, staff development opportunities, and an increase in the number of staff contributing to leadership roles. Again, the importance of a clear focus for partnership efforts was underlined, though here successful areas of focus extended beyond the development of teaching and learning. Successful partnerships leant heavily on the skills of the 'case manager'—generally an outsider who brings new skills and a wider perspective to the partnerships. But, 'brokerage' was also important—the capacity to initiate links and access support. Though case managers played an important role here, it was noticeable that others, too, developed brokerage skills. Facilitation was a similar issue. Partnerships need to be facilitated—setting them up is not enough—but there a range of staff who can grow into facilitation roles. The report points out, however, that sustainability remains an issue; it seems likely that partnerships will need to be 'renewed' if they are to be sustained, perhaps through the renegotiation of points of focus. Nevertheless, it could be argued that sustained improvement and sustained partnerships are not the same thing, and so long as the one is maintained, perhaps we should not be concerned if the other turns out to be a series of short-term engagements, rather than a marriage.

One of the key advantages of collaborative networks compared to other forms of school improvement, such as externally led school improvement programmes, is that it allows schools to co-construct improvement around individual school needs, rather than buying into programmes that may not be properly contextualised (Datnow, Hubbard, & Mehan, 2002). Similarly, it can help solve the problem of purely internal improvement programmes that may flounder due to the lack of internal capacity in schools. The fact that networks co-construct their own solutions rather than simply implementing externally developed programmes is advantageous in that it leads to active construction of knowledge, and therefore stronger learning than is possible in a buy-in situation. However, this can also be a slower process than adopting external reforms, and can lead to an element of reinventing existing solutions and susceptibility to educational fads. However, buy-in is unlikely to generate new knowledge in the way that collaborative learning has been found to do in successful instances (Ainscow & West, 2006). There is evidence in a number of studies that this collaborative learning can indeed increase school capacity (Chapman & Allen, 2005), can help forge relationships across previously isolated schools (Harris et al., 2005), and they can therefore be an effective means of sharing good practice (Harris et al., 2005; Datnow et al., 2002). The extent to which this actually happens in existing collaborations is variable, however, some finding that real sharing of practice can be limited (Lindsay, Harris, Chapman, & Muijs, 2005). Ainscow and West (2005) report that collaboration leads to teachers viewing disadvantaged pupils in new ways, and to lesser polarisation between schools. However, we need to be careful to easily assume that learning can occur or that competencies can merely be transferred from one school to another. Competencies are both contextual and embedded, in the sense that they are ultimately located in people and culture. This means that ongoing intervention will be required before sharing is possible, and that a shared language needs to be developed between the partners (Nooteboom, 2004).

As well as these advantages, collaborations can sometimes be entered into for reasons that are not related to improving performance. Ego and empire building on the part of senior managers may be one of the reasons for taking on leadership within a federation, for example, as are the desire for a 'new challenge' on the part of managers. Added prestige by allying to another school seen as more successful or higher status can also be seen as a cause for collaboration (Borgatti & Foster, 2003). External coercion may be another reason for entering into collaboration.

1.3 Structure of This Book

There is therefore some promising evidence of the strength of networking and collaboration, though it is limited in scope. There is also growing evidence of the conditions required for effective networking and collaboration.

One aspect that has not been explored in any depth, however, is the theoretical background to networking and collaboration. Therefore, in Part I of this book we will look at theoretical positions on networking between organisations, with a view to informing both research and practical decision making. In Chapter 2 we will discuss networking and collaboration as a public policy framework, looking at the reasons why collaboration and networking have become increasingly popular public service delivery mechanisms, and what research on non-educational parts of the public sector can teach us. In Chapter 3 we will discuss localised theories of networking and collaboration, in particular constructivist organisational theory, social capital theory, and social network theory. In Chapter 4 we will look at societal theories of networking and collaboration, like the theory of New Social Movements, Durkheimian notions of networking, and anomie and functionalist organisational theories. In Chapter 5 we will develop a typology of social networks.

In Part II we will take a more practical look at research on existing networks and collaborative arrangements, and will present a range of research studies of collaboratives and networks. In Chapters 6 and 7 we will discuss federations of schools, a form of networking that has been officially sanctioned and become popular in England over recent years. In Chapter 6 we will focus on qualitative evidence on governance, management, and school improvement, and in Chapter 7 on quantitative evidence of impact on performance. In Chapter 8 we will look at a longitudinal study of collaboration at school district or local authority level, while in Chapter 9 we focus on collaboration in rural areas. Finally, in Chapter 10 of this part, we will look at collaboration between schools and external agencies in so-called multiagency contexts.

In Part III we will look in more depth at what conditions and processes may help us to develop successful collaborative networks. In Chapter 11 we will draw some general conclusions from a decade of research on networking and collaboration conducted by the authors. In Chapter 12 we will look at internal conditions for effective collaboration. In Chapter 13 we will look at external conditions and constraints, while in Chapter 14 we will discuss leadership issues in networks.

Part I
Theories and Backgrounds

Chapter 2
Networking and Collaboration as a Public Policy Framework

As we mentioned in Chapter 1, networking and collaboration have become increasingly popular mechanisms for the delivery of public policy over the past two decades. In this chapter we will explore some of the backgrounds to this evolution.

2.1 The Development of Networks as Policy Delivery Mechanisms

In this chapter we will therefore present an overview of international policy initiatives aimed at promoting collaboration in education. We will then frame these within broader public sector policy, drawing on models positing networking as the new framework of public policy more generally. We will discuss the background to these changes in public policy, implications thereof, and the role of education policy in this.

Over recent years management of the public sector has become increasingly devolved from central government in many countries. In countries like the US and the UK, the central government is less inclined than in the past to directly run public services, preferring to devolve services to lower levels of government, and, more often, to develop partnerships and collaborations with private and public sector organisations, in many cases charities. Government has increasingly become a commissioner of services, and a partner in delivery networks rather than a deliverer itself (Milward & Provan, 2003).

The increase in multiagency and multi-partner work is in part the result of a view that sees these as being able to result in greater use of common local resources, and the ability to take collective action. This is most likely to be successful where transaction costs (the cost of setting up and maintaining the network) are low and the benefits to individuals and organisations involved are high, and where resources are scarce, as is frequently the case in the public sector (Berry et al., 2004). A perceived increase in the complexity of problems government has to deal with is likewise seen as contributing to this trend. Increasingly, government managers are no longer primarily in charge of managing large bureaucracies in a hierarchical manner, but are instead managing resources and relationships between providers of the resources needed to fulfill particular policy goals (Goldsmith & Eggers, 2004). The perceived

D. Muijs et al., *Collaboration and Networking in Education*,
DOI 10.1007/978-94-007-0283-7_2,

benefits of networking in the public sector are multiple, and include, according to Lawson (2004) effectiveness gains, efficiency gains, resource gains (such as savings and increases in resourcing), capacity gains, and legitimacy gain.

Therefore, networks have become increasingly common in public sector management. McGuire and Agranoff (2007, p. 1) define such networks as *A public management network includes agencies involved in a public policy making and/or administrative structure through which public goods and services may be planned, designed, produced, and delivered.*

The growth of networks is taking two main forms in public policy. The first is the increased use of private sector partners in the delivery of services. Such networks have become widespread as policy delivery has increasingly been devolved to various quasi-governmental agencies, who, in turn, work with local networks to fill in capacity gaps in their own organisations. This is seen by many commentators as essential in light of the growing complexity of the issues that government and its agencies need to address, and of the increasing demands being made by the public with regard to the quality and choice of public services offered to them (Goldsmith & Eggers, 2004), a factor that is certainly obvious in the increased emphasis on educational and school quality in popular discourse and the press in many countries. The private sector is seen as more efficient and effective, and more responsive to consumer demand than traditional bureaucratic public sector organisations.

The second key form of networking is more internally focussed, and involves greater joined-up governance between public sector bodies. Again, this evolution has occurred mainly as a result of the perceived complexity of the issues facing the public sector, in some cases hastened by cases of neglect occurring due to a lack of coordination between different public agencies, such as in the highly publicised 'Baby P' child neglect case in the UK. In the UK in particular, 'joined-up government' has been a theme of recent administrations that have attempted to stop unnecessary overlap and people falling between the cracks created by varying responsibilities of different agencies. An example of this that has had a profound influence on education is the creation of Children's Services at the local government level, that have replaced the old Local Education Authorities with integrated authorities responsible not just for education but also for all social and health services for children across a local authority or district. This was mirrored at the national level in the creation of the Department for Children, Schools and Families to replace the Department for Education and Science that was previously responsible for schools and education policy. Of course, it remains unclear to what extent these efforts can be seen as genuine networks rather than just larger and more centralised bureaucracies, and the future of these structures is uncertain at the time of writing as a new coalition government takes charge in a climate in which budget cuts are essential to safeguard the economic future and health of the country.

These developments are seen to have been aided by the development of digital technology, which, as well as allowing for ever greater volumes of information to be collected and stored, also allows for easier communication and sharing of information between agencies and organisations, be it in the form of electronic communication or in the form of shared or jointly accessible databases (Goldsmith & Eggers, 2004). The creation of large electronic databases is therefore another characteristic feature of recent changes in governance. The National Pupil Database in England, for example, collects pupil achievement on statutory tests as well as background data such as ethnicity and eligibility for Free School Meals. As each pupil gets a Unique Pupil Number, they can be tracked over time, with the possibility of additional data being added.

2.2 Types of Public Policy Networks

Two main motivations appear to underlie the formation of networks in the public sector. In one set of cases, a charismatic leader of one of the organisations involved, or an external political actor, will take action to set up the network in light of perceived advantages of networks, deficiencies in current organisational structures or personal ambition and empire-building. In other cases networks are formed specifically to carry out a particular project or function that would be hard to do for any individual organisation. Again, changes in policies and priorities on the part of the government often underlie these networks (Agranoff, 2006). Sometimes networks can develop more organically in response to perceived client needs, especially where there is limited perceived overlap in functions between the organisations in the network.

Goldsmith and Eggers (2004) identify five main types of public sector networks, many relating to public–private partnerships (PPP):

- Service contracts, in which the government or its agencies essentially go into a contractual relationship with other public or private sector organisations to provide goods or services;
- Supply chain networks, where a complex product delivery mechanism is set up with private sector partners;
- Ad hoc networks, set up in response to a particular need or crisis, such as fighting an infectious disease and informing the public about it;
- Channel partnerships, in which partner organisations act as disseminators of goods or services for government;
- Information dissemination partnerships, where government partners with public or private partners to disseminate information to the public; and
- Civic switchboard, where the government connects organisations to create network to deliver particular services to the public.

This typology seems overly government-led however, and ignores the many networks of public sector organisations that have come about without direct government intervention or with the goal of delivering services that are not directly government-mandated.

Sullivan and Skelcher (2002) identify three types of public sector network:

- Contractual relationships, which are similar to Goldsmith & Eggers Service Contracts
- Networks, which in contrast to contractual relationships are informal rather than legally binding, are based on personal relationships and are fluid in nature
- Partnerships, which the authors describe as collaboration through joint decision making and production, and involve different agencies negotiating shared goals and committed to working together for long term. It is the latter which would most commonly describe educational networks.

Networks can also be distinguished based on the extent to which they are located within the public sector, are collaborations between state and non-profit charitable organisations, or form collaborations between public and private sector organisations.

Within-public sector networks have traditionally been most common, and often emerge as a reaction to a perceived fragmentation of services delivered by organisations responsible to different governmental bodies. For example, Health and Social services typically resort under separate government ministries and are delivered by different institutions. In view of the many services such as health prevention that are more usefully seen as partnerships between health and social services, joint networks are increasingly being set up to deliver specific programmes between the two. The goal of this type of collaboration is primarily to provide a better level of service and overcome the problem of overspecialisation that may hinder effective provision (Nylen, 2007). Although in principal such governmental and quasi-governmental organisations should work together relatively seamlessly in the light of the oft-stated preference for integrated policy and delivery, this is frequently not the case, as differences in organisational culture can be every bit as strong as between private and public sector organisations, and differences in accounting and accountability structures between different government ministries make networking problematic. In many cases it appears that government agencies are more constrained in terms of adapting structures and procedures to networking and collaboration than many private organisations.

An increasingly popular form of networking consists of networks between public sector bodies and not-for-profit charitable organisations. This form of collaboration has been particularly popular with right of centre governments, who see this as a way of bypassing what they consider to be the inefficiencies of government agencies by harnessing the dynamism of charitable organisations, which are also seen as having better direct contacts with the people particular programmes are trying to reach. An example of this is the important role played by churches and community groups alongside local government in rehousing efforts after the Katrina disaster, which provides an example of successful networking between public and charitable organisations, delivering many of the benefits that were hoped for by its proponents (Airriess, Li, Leong, Chen, & Keith, 2007). Obviously, as with other forms of networking, there are examples where this form of collaboration has been less successful. Typically, in these cases cultural differences may lie at the heart of problems, especially the emphasis of many government agencies on targets and accountability, which is not always shared by charitable organisations. The increased bureaucracy that goes along with this type of collaboration may well stretch the means of smaller charities, and may lead to some charity workers feeling compromised.

Probably the greatest growth of collaboration has been in the area of public–private partnerships. This has become a preferred mode of delivery of a wide range of government projects, from large-scale infrastructure development to small-scale evaluations of social government programmes. Benefits of this are seen to lie in harnessing the efficiency and dynamism of the private sector to deliver public projects, bringing in management expertise from the private sector, and delivering co- (or in some cases, full) financing of projects that would otherwise be problematic from the standpoint of government budgets. As many of these projects have long-term implications (for example in terms of management of buildings funded by private partners), it is in many cases too early to fully judge the effectiveness of this approach, while in Europe recent crackdowns by Eurostat (the European Union's official statistics agency) on the notion of PPP projects being off-budget for governments may make this approach less attractive to government for their large-scale construction projects. Economic and financial difficulties may make private companies less interested in this for networking as well. Obviously, cultural differences are evident here, and one criticism of PPP in education has been that public sector managers lack the contract expertise of their private sector counterparts, leading to unbalanced costs and benefits of such collaborations.

Another distinction to be made is between situations where collaboration leads to *pooled interdependence,* where each provider contributes one part to the overall approach, *sequential interdependence,* where one organisations' services are linked with those of another, and *reciprocal interdependence,* where organisations' provisions are closely intertwined to the extent that, in many cases, the collaboration will prove very hard to unravel (Goldsmith & Eggers, 2004).

In education we can see examples of all these types of collaboration. Collaboration with other organisations from the public sector is frequent. Where full-service or extended provision exists schools work with health and social services, police and other public sector institutions. Collaboration with other schools, which will form the bulk of the content of this book, is again an example of collaboration with other public service institutions. Collaboration with charitable organisations is less frequent, though clearly does exist. Schools frequently collaborate with churches, and sexual health charities to deliver various programmes in schools. Collaboration with the private sector has become increasingly prevalent, and takes a number of forms. Public–private partnerships have become common in education in some countries, such as England, where the 'Building Schools for the Future' initiative has led to a strong emphasis on building new schools where the private sector part finances construction, and in return typically retains a contract to service the building once completed. Other forms of partnership with private sector organisations exist. Schools may work with local businesses to provide enterprise education, or have particular activities, such as sports, sponsored. A particular form of partnership is where private partners sponsor or set up a school as a whole. This is the case, for example, in the Academies programme in England or the free schools initiative in Sweden. Here, schools may be set up by private individuals or companies (in England only on a non-profit basis, in Sweden potentially for profit). In some cases this type of initiative can veer towards privatisation rather than private-public networking.

2.3 Research on Public Sector Networking

Many benefits have been posited for networking and collaboration in the private sector. Networking is seen to encourage experimentation, by allowing different organisations or providers to come up with a range of solutions from which government can then pick the most appropriate one. Networking is seen as allowing greater flexibility and opportunities to tailor products and services to the needs of clients and client groups better than would be possible in a centralised bureaucracy, and networking allows government and its agencies to focus on their core business while contracting out services to partners who are better able to deliver specialised services, specialisation being problematic for centralised systems (Goldsmith & Eggers, 2004).

This variety of forms of collaboration obviously makes it hard to reach general conclusions about the effectiveness of collaboration. Rather, it is necessary to study different forms of collaboration between different types of actors and look at the effectiveness of these forms separately. This inevitably means that some types of collaboration have been subject to more and more rigorous research than others, leading to gaps in our knowledge base.

One area that has received considerable attention is that of interagency collaboration in the Health sector. There is considerable evidence of not only effectiveness of collaboration in delivering improved health outcomes, but also of the difficulties and costs in achieving these outcomes. The cost benefit equation in particular is one that requires careful attention, as, especially when formal structures are set up the extent of the cost requires significant and measurable benefits to make the effort worthwhile. There is, however, evidence that a degree of formalisation is necessary to increase effectiveness (Nylen, 2007).

Benefits accrue from the preventive effect of merging the knowledge of different health providers, both in terms of clients and treatments. Innovation can also be a positive consequence of collaboration, as in some cases entirely new treatments have resulted from collaboration, that couldn't have been delivered by one agency on its own. Efficiency savings are a sometimes underestimated but therefore no less important benefit of collaboration.

Nylen (2007) distinguishes three kinds of strategies for collaboration between agencies in the healthcare sector: commitment-based networking relies on trust and informal relationships, and is a low-cost strategy, though not easy to achieve. It has potentially strong benefits, though is prone to collapse due to changed personal circumstances of actors involved. Assignment reallocation strategy is focussed on setting up formal structures. This strategy requires limited resources, but, according to Nyles, has at most medium potential benefits. Finally, Formalised team building requires both formal structures and the development of intensive relationships and trust. This strategy has high costs, but high potential benefits.

While potentially beneficial, networks can also hold considerable risks as deliverers of public policy. Firstly, poor performance by any organisation involved in the network can lead the network as a whole to underperform and fail in the delivery of essential services. Quality assurance and monitoring progress to network goals in all participating organisations is therefore a key management challenge for networks and collaboratives. Failed oversight is often a factor in instances where collaboration has failed, especially in models of outsourcing services to the private sector (Goldsmith & Eggers, 2004). Contract management is important here, and one problem in many public–private collaborations is the lack of expertise in drawing up contracts of this nature in some public sector organisations, which has left them with many of the costs and the private partners with most of the benefits of the collaborative project. The level of resources required to set up collaboration and the additional workload that can be involved for staff in partner organisations are other potential problems, as is the fact that it can take quite a long time to reach decisions or goals due to the negotiation processes between different network partners (Sullivan & Skelcher, 2002). Power imbalances between different network partners can lead to tensions.

Managing the network also becomes key to solving some of the other risks and weaknesses of network approaches. Cultural differences may hinder communication, while goal incongruence may lead to major misunderstandings, as has been found to be the case in many collaborations between schools and social services, for example. As well as different goals, different levels of information between partners in a network may cause problems, and again lead to unequal gains and cost across partners, which is likely to result in a breakdown of trust and a consequent lessening of effective collaborative work in the network. Networks in the public sector have from time to time run into severe capacity problems, especially with regard to managing the network. In many cases network management has not been part of the training or career path of civil servants, who consequently struggle with this (Goldsmith & Eggers, 2004).

2.4 Collaboration as an Educational Policy

In education, the last decades have, in many countries, seen a greater emphasis on competition rather than collaboration in education. In England, in many ways at the forefront of these developments, the introduction of School-Based Management, greater parental choice, school 'League Tables', in which newspapers publish publicly available school performance data, and a bidding culture where an increased part of school funding is obtained through competitive bidding processes have all conspired to create a climate of competition over the past decades. Similar moves towards a greater emphasis on competition between schools have been seen in countries like Sweden, where regulation in the 1990s made it relatively easy for groups of parents, charities, or education businesses to set up schools and where parental choice was introduced, and the US with the set-up of Charter schools and various local experiments with school vouchers through which parents can, again, exercise choice. This has very much been a deliberate strategy, based on the premise that, as in the private sector, competition between schools will lead to greater efficiency and effectiveness in the sector. This has always been a disputed position in education, however, with many commentators arguing that key differences with private sector organisations exist. One of these lies in the consequences of failure. While in the private sector failure of businesses is seen as a form of creative destruction, whereby capital gets reallocated to more efficient enterprises or to sectors where the country enjoys a competitive advantage without harming consumers (whether this is also true of employees is of course another matter), the same is not true of schools. For a school to fail due to the competitive pressures from, say, a newly built trust school in the area is highly problematic, however. Children will still have received their education from this school, have been taught by demoralised teachers, in a class full of demoralised pupils where peer support for education is not available, and will not have a second chance at education in most cases (Muijs, 2006a). There is also evidence that one of the effects of competition is that where some schools improve, others serving the same area may worsen, largely due to a redistribution of pupils between schools, as the effective school attracts more aspirational parents and pupils and is able to divest itself of the hardest to teach, who end up in other neighbourhood schools (West, 2008). This is obviously highly problematic from an equity point of view, and it is therefore not surprising that even during those periods in which education systems have most strongly emphasised competition, collaboration between schools has continued. Wallace (1998), for example, describes voluntary collaborations between schools under the very free-market oriented conservative government of the early to mid 1990s as aimed at joint work for joint purposes, and usually as at least in part aiming to reduce competition between schools in a particular area. He sees the continued existence of these collaborations as a form of deliberate resistance to government policy and as creating an alternative policy space not only as a form of resistance to dominant policy, but also as a survival mechanism.

More recently these competition-based policies have been supplemented (though not replaced) by policies encouraging collaboration, for example through Education action Zones aimed at improving schools across local areas of disadvantage, or Networked Learning Communities where schools collaborate together to innovate. These policy changes have been strongly focussed on school improvement, the principle being that schools can learn from one another. In recent years there has also been an increased emphasis, at least in England, on schools collaborating with other agencies for the purpose of serving the so-called 'whole child', thus forming partnerships with other (usually state) agencies.

All these developments therefore clearly parallel to those happening in other parts of the public sector as described above. From this, it follows that schools and educational actors and policymakers can learn from other parts of the public sector, especially on matters such as which types of collaboration work (and, as we have seen, there are clear examples of success from the Health sector and local government), and what factors can aid or hinder collaboration. Of particular concern here are the issues of cultural differences and of contractual differences reported above. These are likely to come to the fore in education as well, not just where schools collaborate with other agencies, where cultural differences may be particularly strong, or with the private sector, where contractual differences have proven to be particularly problematic, but also in school-to-school collaborations where different schools often find it hard to agree on values and goals, may find it hard to learn from one another, and where a lack of contractual agreements can easily lead to misunderstandings and, ultimately, the falling apart of the collaborative or network. All these factors will be discussed more extensively in later chapters in this book. First, we will have a look at what the theoretical bases may be for collaboration in education.

Chapter 3
Localised Theories of Networking and Collaboration

In this and the next chapter we will explore the theoretical basis for networking in education. To do this, we will draw primarily on theories developed outside of an educational context, but will discuss the educational applications of the theoretical frameworks mentioned. In this chapter we will look at more localised theories, in the following chapter at more societally grounded ones.

There is a long tradition of psychological research on collaboration and networks. In this chapter we will discuss the main findings and theories from psychological research, such as social network theory, social learning theory, and constructivist organisational theory. The applicability of these theories to education will be discussed along with the ways they can illuminate practice in this area.

3.1 Constructivist Organisational Theory as a Basis for Networking

According to constructivist theory, organisations are sense-making systems creating shared perceptions and interpretations of reality. This means that each organisation will to a certain extent have its own unique perception of reality, albeit one that is anchored in its context (organisations are thus not free to construct an unanchored reality without failing). This sense-making function is essential for organisations to function effectively, but runs the risk of becoming myopic, in that this shared perception of reality may be closed to external influences leading to a disconnection with alternative realities and the organisation's environment. It is this myopia that can be addressed through networking with other organisations or other external partners that can provide access to a complementary cognition (Weick, 1995). This 'myopia problem' also means that the more uncertainty and complexity exist in the environment, the more there is a need for collaboration to ensure that organisations are able to adopt the necessary competence to cope with the complexity that surrounds and impacts on them (Nooteboom, 2004). This would certainly appear to be the case in education, and particularly for schools serving disadvantaged communities.

While linked to constructivist organisational theory this is by no means a new finding. Communication across different groups has long been stated as being key to the development of new ways of thinking and even democracy, John Stuart Mill

D. Muijs et al., *Collaboration and Networking in Education*,
DOI 10.1007/978-94-007-0283-7_3,

(1859) for example pointing to the fact that a lack of communication between different viewpoints limits the possibility of the development of truth, while Ahrendt (1968) pointed similarly to the need to ponder a range of others' views to come to more valid decisions. The idea is therefore that exposure to different viewpoints generates both greater understanding of one's own viewpoints (through the need to actually rationalise them) and greater awareness of rationales of others, and appropriate change to ones' own viewpoints. Contact between groups (or, by extension, organisations) can therefore lead to 'deprovincialisation', whereby people learn that their norms, behaviours, and habits are but one of many possible ways of dealing with the world, and

The constructivist view of the organisation is connected to Vygotskian views of learning. Vygotsky posited that co-operation lies at the basis of learning, through the way in which interaction leads to scaffolding that allows actors to achieve more than they would be able to do individually (Vygotsky, Vygotsky, & John-Steiner, 1978). Knowledge for Vygotsky, like for Piaget, is embodied in actions and interactions with the environment and others. In this sense, organisations are most likely to be effective learners where they form communities of practice in networks or other collaborative arrangements, and are engaged in a process of social learning that occurs when actors who have a common interest in some subject or problem collaborate to share ideas, find solutions, and build innovations. This view of collaborative ventures as communities of practice therefore presupposes that new knowledge emerges as groups working together towards the achievement of joint goals (Borgatti & Foster, 2003).

However, as organisations have complementary cognitions and a different sense of reality, collaboration, while often necessary, is by no means straightforward. In order for learning and growth to occur, collaborating organisations need to have sufficient cognitive distance for new insights to emerge, but at the same time need to be similar enough for dialogue to be possible and constructive (Nooteboom, 2004). This is similar to findings from political science that show that exposure to difference and different world views can lead to conflict rather than tolerance if people haven't got to know one another prior to political conversation (thus reducing cognitive distance), though, conversely, political tolerance is linked to greater levels of interpersonal contact, and in particular to more interpersonal affective ties, with individuals with differing views in some studies (Mutz, 2002). These ties, will, however, tend to be weaker in nature than those with whom greater agreement exists, suggesting that a greater number of weak ties may be more effective in bridging cognitive gaps than a small number of strong ties.

A factor that complicates both the construction and study of networks is the fact that, certainly in networks of individuals, roles are strongly contextually defined. As shown in the studies by the Manchester Anthropologists in the 1950s and 1960s, structural arrangements can only explain very partially the different roles actors play in networks. Much is explained by contextual factors that are particularistic and local, such as relationships, history, and power (Berry et al., 2004). This is important in the sense that relationships within a network will be in part determined by the particularistic relations between individuals in each organisation interacting with one another, but also in that relations between organisations themselves may be strongly localistic and individual, determined by the kind of historical and contextual factors that shape local conditions.

Constructivist organisational theory can clearly be linked to moves towards creating schools as learning communities, in that from the constructivist point of view this effort may be more successful if carried out by schools collaborating in a network rather than by schools acting alone. School networks can therefore be said to fall within this model when they are formed primarily with the goal of knowledge creation, and are constructed in such a way as to allow optimal openness and collaboration. Joint CPD, regular contacts between staff across schools and from all levels of the school hierarchy, and relationships based on the view that all schools in the network have a valuable contribution to make would characterise this type of network.

3.2 Creating Social Capital as a Basis for Networking

A related theory on the importance of networking focuses on the value of networking and collaboration in creating social capital. Social capital contains three main elements:

1. Resources embedded in a social context,
2. Resources that are accessed or mobilised, and
3. Resources in purposive action (Lin, 1999).

The value of networking in this perspective is seen as lying in its ability to harness resources held by other actors and increase the flow of information in a network. Furthermore, a network can exert more influence on its social and political surroundings than individual actors (Lin, 1999). Social capital can also help spread innovation, which, according to Hargreaves (2004) is best done through bottom-up networks, that can both quickly link schools to innovators, and may themselves lead to innovations that are more open to change and challenge and less likely to ossify than top-down strategies. Both of these factors are evidenced by the finding that strategic alliances are particularly common in R&D intensive sectors where knowledge is particularly important, and that firms where there is a greater breadth of knowledge necessary to produce their products, there is a greater likelihood to form alliances with other firms (Grant & Baden-Fuller, 2004).

Knowledge lies in different minds, both individual and collective, and therefore networks are needed to increase effectiveness. The value of networking lies in spanning 'structural holes' where information or skills are lacking (Burt, 1992). This makes collaboration a potentially fruitful strategy for all actors involved in a network, as each may in theory be able to span structural holes, something which becomes more likely when a network consists of several actors. In this view, networking can be unsuccessful where there is too strong an imbalance between actors in terms of what information/skills they posses, or where structural ties can imprison actors in negative behaviour patterns (Borgatti & Foster, 2003). This mutually beneficial view of alliances is hared by researchers who have looked specifically at organisational learning in business organisations, where the goal of collaboration is to acquire knowledge from collaborating partners, though some emphasis has been placed on differences in terms of speed of learning among different collaborators, suggesting unequal benefits in terms of learning (Grant & Baden-Fuller, 2004).

A key distinction in social capital theory therefore lies in whether the gains from the network accrue mainly to the individual school, the network as a whole, society or a combination of these. In the most successful examples of networking, social capital is both an individual and a collective good. This is important, as in cases where the benefits are seen as entirely societal or at network level, the motivation of individual actors (schools) may be limited. On the other hand, purely individual benefits may tempt actors to play zero sum games, thus limiting trust and eventually causing the demise of the network (Lin, 1999). Importantly, gains from network activity are not just accrued through physical resources. Rather, the embeddedness that network membership entails means networks go beyond pure market relationships, providing specific opportunities through the trust that develops. In particular, 'thicker information' on strategy and know-how becomes possible, and may lead to joint problem-solving arrangements, and the development of voluntary exchanges (Uzzi, 1996). This is clearly important in educational settings in which competition and school choice are used as accountability mechanisms, where networks may provide a countervailing force to the centripetal forces of competition. This embeddedness tends to start with reciprocal interactions, aimed very specifically at reciprocal advantage gains, which over time develops into relationships of trust over the course of successful interactions. This initial interaction and exchange is itself facilitated where an initial stock of trust exists as a result of previous relations and exchanges. Networks can then be extended through personal recommendation and third-party relationships, as network members make introductions to others. It is therefore clear, that in the private sector at least, such networks can be highly personal, and can lead to a greater focus on cultivating long-term relationships as opposed to being focussed on short-term gains (Uzzi, 1996). It is therefore clear that networks can benefit organisational survival through the enhanced access they provide to information and support, greater than what would be likely in purely market-based relationships. However, over time there is a danger of networks becoming overly inward-looking, interactions occurring mainly within the network, which can in itself lead to a decrease in innovation. Furthermore, there is a danger that emotional ties may override rational considerations. Therefore, Uzzi (1996) in his study of network ties in the garment industry in New York, recommends a mixture of arms-length economic ties and embedded network ties for organisational survival.

One aspect of this is the importance of the position of the organisation in the network, with greater centrality allowing control of resources and, as a result of this, power (Uzzi, 1996). Some have even argued that 'hub' organisations can control the network, though more recently it has generally come to be understood that total control of one organisation over the actions of others is impossible as well as undesirable (Ritter, Wilkinson, & Johnston, 2003).

It is clear that the majority of work in this perspective has focussed quite strongly on the aspect of knowledge acquisition. Some researchers, however, see this emphasis as erroneous and claim that the main benefits of collaboration lie at least as strongly in implementation, if not more so. Grant and Baden-Fuller (2004) see this as the main goal of collaboration, claiming that a view that sees collaboration as aimed at gaining ever-increasing knowledge is incompatible with trends that have seen a greatly increased emphasis on focus and specialisation (and it can be said that this emphasis on a clear focus is one that is also strongly present in the school effectiveness perspective that has been influential in education over the past decades). For both collaborating partners (in a dichotomy) to learn all each other's knowledge would be inefficient. This is especially the case where a great deal of different types of knowledge is required, which becomes inefficient to produce within the organisation. Rather, what is needed is to use the other's specialised knowledge without having to fully acquire it oneself. Obviously, this will be more strongly the case the more the organisations fundamentally differ from one another in terms of their own specialised knowledge. In schools, which fundamentally are engaged in similar activity requiring similar skills and knowledge, this may not appear to be the case. However, it is applicable to those situations where schools collaborate with other agencies, for example social services, to address problems that children may have that may impede learning. Furthermore, it may lead us to question the extent to which it may be more profitable for schools to offer different specialised curriculum areas, for example catering and metalworking.

Collaborations in this perspective are more strongly driven by clearly worked out self-interest than in the constructivist model. The goals of networking from this perspective would lie mainly in knowledge transfer or the acquisition of increased influence or voice within schools' (political) community. Where the goal is the former, schools are likely to be working together because of perceived different strengths and weaknesses, and may develop specialisms further through collaboration, such as offering courses to their students in different partner schools that have capacity in that area. Full-Service Extended Schools, where schools team up with other providers to offer services they cannot provide on their own, may in many cases be another example of this model. This perspective points to the need for a rational decision-making process in terms of whether or not to collaborate that is based primarily on the self-interest of the actors, as well as on the transaction costs involved. The different levels of difficulty in acquiring different types of knowledge (e.g. acquiring tacit knowledge is far harder and will necessitate far more intensive and long-term collaboration than explicit knowledge) will play a key role in that decision-making process.

What both the social capital and constructivist organisational theories tend to somewhat understate and underestimate, is the extent to which networks can not only pool or share knowledge, but can also be instrumental in developing new knowledge through experimentation. Because collaboration and networking allows organisations to explore different configurations and ideas, horizons get broadened and the opportunity for new thinking and strategies to develop may occur. A disposition of greater openness and acceptance of difference that can result from collaboration is particularly important to this. In that way, networks can become more than the sum of their parts, and develop into something new (Goldsmith & Eggers, 2004). Examples of this clearly exist in school-to-school collaborations. Teachers coming together to discuss pedagogy in their subject often end up not just learning from each other, but developing new practices through discussion, and practise in peer tutoring groups.

3.3 Social Network Theory as a Basis for Networking

Another influential theory is Social network theory. This is a theory originating in social psychology, which has explored the ways in which social networks form, and has been very influential in organisational studies, contributing a large part of the vocabulary we use when discussing organisational networks.

Social network theory originates in the analysis of social relationships, and sees these relationships as key towards understanding human (and organisational) behaviour. These social relationships between individuals are described as consisting of *nodes,* which are the individual actors, and *ties,* which are the relationships that bind them. These relationships are varied in type, and can be anything from family ties to mutual dislikes or financial exchange relationships. According to Dunn (1983, p. 454) social network theory makes four basic assumptions:

1. Knowledge structures and processes are constituted by relations among persons, objects, events, and actions and not by attributes of individuals (such as policymakers) or categoric entities (such as agencies, states, and countries).
2. Relations are structured, with structures viewed as regularities in the patterns of relations among concrete entities. These can be distinguished from covariant properties (such as size, centralisation, and differentiation) of categoric entities.
3. Structured relations involve overt behavioural properties (for example, frequency of direct contact) as well as cognitive ones (such as congruence of beliefs, orientations, and meanings).
4. Behavioural and cognitive properties emerge from structured relations, including symbolically meaningful transactions and exchanges; relations are not intrinsic properties of individual or categoric entities. The organisation of social relations thus becomes a central concept in analysing the structural properties of the networks within which individual actors are embedded, and for detecting emergent social phenomena that have no existence at the level of the individual actor.

Research on social networks often takes the form of mappings of relationships between nodes, using social network maps. An example of such a map is given in Fig. 3.1.

In this figure the nodes are denoted by a dot (e.g. ×38) and the ties by a line. Data on ties can be collected in a number of ways, for example by asking pupils in a classroom to nominate their three best friends, or by asking teachers to nominate

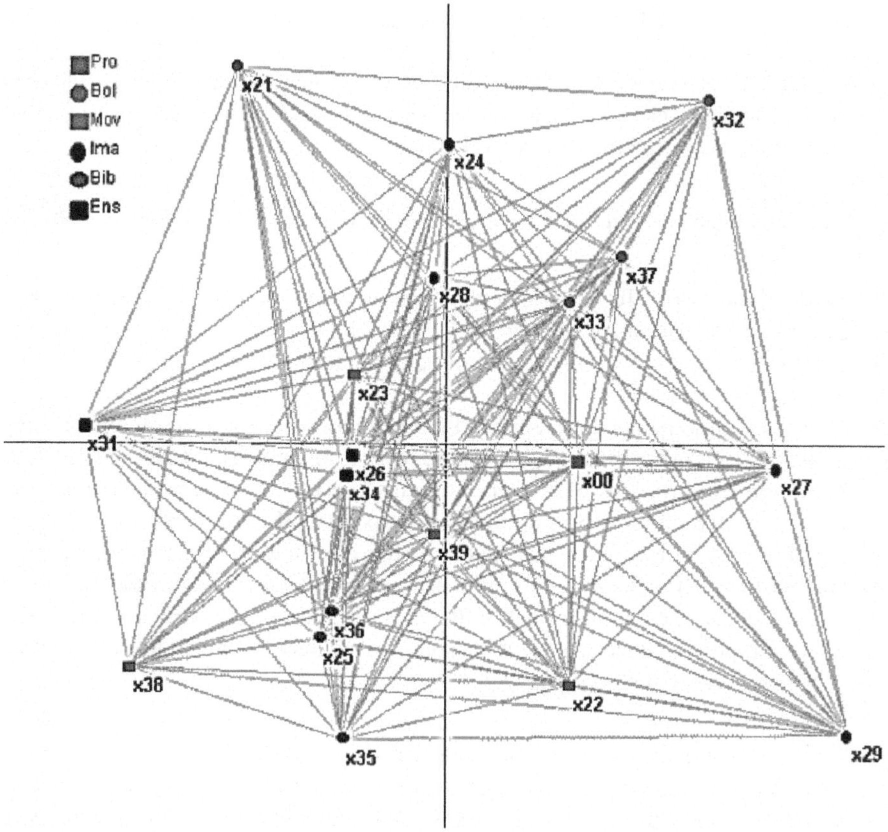

Fig. 3.1 A social network in a school (from Martinez, Dimitriadis, Rubia, Gomez, & de la Fuente, 2003, p. 365)

which colleagues they go to for advice on teaching. There are two main types of networks studied using this approach: whole networks, encompassing all the ties that make up a particular network, or personal networks, where one looks at all the ties from the standpoint of an individual node.

This form of analysis has applications across a wide range of fields, including the study of organisations. Organisations, in this perspective, can be considered to be social groupings with relatively stable patterns of interaction over time (Tichy, Tushman, & Fombrun, 1979). Work in organisations has led to knowledge on the type of ties that may predominate within them and the characteristics of networks within and between organisations. In particular, three properties of networks are deemed important (Tichy et al., 1979):

- Transactional Content: Content that is exchanged between nodes. For example, two employees may exchange information.
- The Nature of the Links: This property can refer to either the strength or the qualitative nature of the relation between nodes. Intensity of the links and reciprocity

between nodes are two examples of the type of information sought in social network analyses.
- Structural Characteristics: The overall pattern of relationships between the system's actors. For instance, clustering, network density, and the existence of special nodes in the network are all structural characteristics.

Structural characteristics can, according to Tichy et al. (1979, p. 509), be divided into four levels:

1. External network: To what extent is the network or organisation linked to external organisations or actors?
2. Total internal network: Given a set of actors that make up the network, in what ways are they linked?
3. Clusters within the network: Areas of the network where actors are more closely linked to each other than they are to the rest of the network are termed clusters. There are various types of clusters: formally prescribed work groups, emergent coalitions, and cliques. A coalition is a temporary alliance of actors who come together for a limited purpose. Cliques are more permanent informal associations and exist for a broader range of purposes – e.g., task, social, and career.
4. Individuals as special nodes within the network: Not all individuals are equally important in social networks, with some being more central and other more peripheral within the network.

Social networks are increasingly being seen as key to the dissemination of innovations. The social networks people are part of are seen as instrumental in whether or not innovations will be adopted, with the likelihood of adoption increasing with the number of members of an actor's network who have already adopted the innovation. Of course, individual characteristics matter too, in that individuals with low innovation thresholds will require fewer members of their social networks to have adopted the innovation before they do than individuals with high innovation thresholds. Again, though, these are related to the network, as this will be the individual's frame of reference, and what will be seen as a high level of adoption may again differ depending on the values and habits in the network (Valente, 1996). This impact of networks on innovation is of course highly relevant to the educational context, in the light of criticism that schools are inherently conservative institutions that have not innovated sufficiently to deal with the major changes in society that have occurred since the initial introduction of mass schooling. Social network theory in this respect points both to opportunities and barriers, the latter linked to limitations within individual networks schools may be part of.

An interesting variation on this type of social network analysis is Actor-Network theory. This sociological theory extends the analysis of networks to society as a whole. The starting point of researchers working in this field is that both traditional and critical sociology has fallaciously posited a social reality that overarches and can explain various forms of human behaviours. This, they posit, is a fallacy that reifies an abstraction and then uses it as an explanation. Rather, sociological analysis in their view needs to start, as it does in social network theory, with the individual and the relationships individuals build with one another. 'Society' results from these ties, as they build up complexly through organisations, and from the deliberate and thoughtful actions of individuals in developing these ties (Latour, 2005).

Social network analysis has clear implications for the study of networks of schools, and this in two distinct areas. Firstly, it is clear that in the same way that we can look at individuals as nodes and their relationships as ties, we can look at individual schools as nodes and their relationships with other schools as ties. More importantly, we can look at the extent to which particular schools are central and peripheral to networks, and clusters within networks. Secondly, social network analysis will allow us to study in some detail what role different individual actors, such as head teachers may play in developing these networks. Again, questions come up of what ties they will have with actors in different schools, how dense the ties are between individuals in different schools, which actors are central to the network and how the network itself relates to external agencies. As mentioned above, some interesting research exists that links networks to innovation. The Actor-Network theory approach meanwhile provides us with a helpful realisation of the need to ground our studies and understanding in the purposeful actions of the individual who are founding, running, and part of networks.

Overall then, the three theoretical approaches discussed in this chapter in their own way provide a compelling case for networking and analysing networks. Constructivist organisational theory, with its strong links to learning and learning organisations, helps us to understand why networks may enhance organisational development through creating communities in which different alternative realities may inform one another, and also provides us with some insights into circumstances under which networks are most likely to work. Social capital theory provides us with a more utilitarian vision of the creation of networks as plugging specific gaps in knowledge and skills through drawing on the strengths of other organisations. Social network theory, meanwhile, provides some very important analysis tools, and allows us to look at networks as essentially links between individuals (or nodes). None of these theories in and of themselves provides us with a full picture of networking and collaboration, however, and all are essentially premised on a relatively localised view of networking. In the next chapter we will explore a number of more societally based theories of networking.

Chapter 4
Societal Theories of Networking and Collaboration

As well as research in psychology, another discipline that has seen a longstanding interest in collaboration and networks is sociology. Key sociological theories of networking and collaboration, including Durkheimian network theory, the theory of new social movements and neo-functionalist theories of networking will be discussed in this chapter. The applicability of these theories to education will be tested along with the ways they can illuminate practice in this area.

4.1 Creating Networks as New Social Movements

New social movements is a term coined to describe the novel forms of social action (such as the environmental movement) that developed from the 1960s onwards. These are seen as far more fluid than traditional social movements (such as Trade Unions), and are characterised not so much by single insurrections as by a series of events, and by organisations/people linked together in various more or less formal and transient patterns. They thus form complex and heterogeneous network structures, in which actors no longer act as individuals but do so in a linked and interdependent way. Actors may have different values and beliefs, but share the common goal of their movement. New social movements are not built on traditional identities around class, ethnicity, or gender, but develop their own collective identity. They are also not constant, but leave structures and cultures behind when they disappear. They are often built around and dominated by activist leaders, and in this way are crucially different from older forms of social movements (Diani, 2003; Hadfield, 2005). New social movements also differ from traditional social movements in a number of other ways. Firstly, they tend to be less dominated by Marxist and socialist ideologies and a pre-occupation on socio-economic matters, and more strongly concerned with issues of identity and quality of life, in many cases the type of issues that are seen to characterise the so-called 'culture wars'. Secondly, they can spring up suddenly, but in some cases can also disappear again. The ecological and gay rights movements are usually cited as typical examples of new social movements, and more recently the anti-globalisation movement that is strongly international in scope, and the US-based 'Tea Party' movements offer good examples of this kind of dynamic (though the latter has not so far been studied as such, probably due to the

D. Muijs et al., *Collaboration and Networking in Education*,
DOI 10.1007/978-94-007-0283-7_4, © Springer Science+Business Media B.V. 2011

more left-wing orientation of most theorists in this field). New social movements are not the same as protest groups, however, as the latter tend to be more localised and single-issue, while NSM's tend to range over quite a large geographical are and range of issues.

New social movements are therefore fundamentally different from traditional social movements in that they both move away from a class-based organisation and move beyond traditional structures through which political conflict is organised, such as political parties and trades unions. Their emergence is often explained as a post-industrial phenomenon, whereby changing societal conditions and in particular the weakening of traditional (social) bonds has led to the development of new forms of identity and new groupings coalescing around these identities (Melucci, 1980). In many cases these movements are focussed as much on symbolic actions intended to change the prevailing culture through awareness raising as on direct action in the political domain. There is often a strong element of self-empowerment in the actions and rhetoric of new social movements. New social movements theory is essentially constructivist, in that, unlike, say, Marxists theories, it stresses the fact that social movements are fragile constructions of the actors involved, and not determined by the structural position of these actors in, for example, the class system (Buechler, 1995). This means that in some cases new social movements may form unlikely alliances between at first sight oppositional groups or people, but whose interests and/or values coalesce in particular ways around particular issues or projects (O'Mahoney & Bechky, 2008). The emergence of new social movements is also often linked to the decline in social bonds in society, which has led to a psychological need for the forging of new bonds, possibly through social movements. Similarly, Heclo (1978) researched 'issue networks' in the US; loose networks of policy experts, academics and writers (such as the recently influential Neo-Conservatives) who form a network with the goal of influencing policy in a particular area.

Looking at the theory of new social movements, it is clear that IT, and in particular the way that the internet allows the development of social networking sites, has aided further the emergence of new social networks. Increasingly, people are forming online communities, and activities are often coordinated and started online. This is a distinguishing theme of a number of recent grassroots and political movements, and may also be of relevance in an educational environment where various forms of Information and Communication Technology (ICT) are becoming ever more central. As Garrett (2006, p. 225) points out: 'By reducing costs associated with publishing and accessing movement information, ICTs have the potential to alter the flow of political information, to reduce the cost of conventional forms of participation, and to create new low-cost forms of participation, ultimately contributing to an upsurge in participation'. However, the extent to which this actually happens, and particularly the depth of this participation are controversial.

Some authors have used new social movements theory in discussions of educational change, though this has typically been done more as a call to action than as a description of a current situation in education. Anyon (2005), for example, claims that the disastrous state of education for the most disadvantaged communities (at least in the US) could (and should) give rise to a new social movement aimed at transforming the education of the most disadvantaged using concepts from critical pedagogy and social justice activism. This she sees as a necessary antidote and reaction to the Neo-Liberal movements that in her view have caused the education of the disadvantaged to be ever more a part of their oppression. She suggests that it should be possible to build up a new social movement comprising disparate groupings of individuals and organisations such as community and education groups for this purpose. Schools themselves, in Anyon's view, can play a role in developing social movements to fight oppression and disadvantage by preparing students to become conscious and engaged in political action. So far, however, this does not seem to have happened to any great extent.

The question is then to what extent the theory of new social movements can be applied to networks of schools. These networks can, according to Hadfield (2005), be classified to some extent as New Social Movements, displaying as they do a number of these characteristics, such as transience, complexity, and the need to build up new identities for the network that are distinct from those of the individual schools (which may, for some schools, be a key motivator to become part of a network). The dominant role of activist leaders can likewise be seen in many school networks. However, a key distinction between New Social Movements and school networks would, for most networks at least, appear to lie in the voluntaristic nature of the alliance. While New Social Movements are formed bottom-up, as a result of perceived common interests, this is the case for only some school networks, many of which have been formed at least in part in reaction to financial incentives or to some form of coercion from higher authorities.

This perspective may provide interesting insights into networks that are bottom-up and values-driven or political in purpose, and the emphasis on the transience of arrangements, the possibility of multiple linkages and the realisation that actors within networks may not fully share values, but may do so only with regard to the goals of the network may provide useful insights into this form of school collaboration. The potential of ICT in collaboration and networking highlighted by some authors in this area is also worthy of further study and development in practice.

This perspective on networks is linked to the view that there is a distinction between intentional and unintentional networks. It is certainly true that both types of networks exist in practice, with more organic and informal contacts growing into networks of schools in some cases. However, the strong policy constraints on schools mean that in many cases these are rendered less significant than formal networks that have been constituted or encouraged within a policy framework in the often over-regulated sphere of education.

4.2 Avoiding Organisational Anomie as a Basis for Collaboration

Another perspective on the importance of collaboration is provided by looking at Durkheimian notions of anomie. Durkheim's key contribution to social sciences was his attempt to explain individual pathologies by reference to social circumstances and factors, and anomie was a key element of his explanation of one of his main research interests, suicide. Looking at data he observed not only high levels of stability in suicide rates in different groups, but also patterns where that rate would rapidly increase or decrease. He related these fluctuations to large-scale societal crises of an economic or political nature often occurring during times of rapid social change and turbulence. In these situations, social control and norms are weakened and values, beliefs, and general norms become fatally weakened (Berkman, Glass, Brisette, & Seeman, 2000). Anomie can be defined as malaise in individuals, characterised by an absence or diminution of standards, and an associated feeling of alienation and purposelessness. Anomie commonly occurs when society has or is undergoing rapid change, and when there is a significant discrepancy between the ideological theories and values individuals and society hold, and their actual practices (Durkheim, 1972). Durkheim distinguishes two forms of anomie: acute or transitory anomie and chronic or institutionalised anomie. Acute anomie is the result of an abrupt temporary change in the circumstances. Chronic anomie results from the fact that the modern world is characterised by continual change and a permanent lack of stability. Durkheim is mainly interested in his second form of anomie which he sees as resulting from the presence in modern culture of a doctrine of constant progress (Besnard, 1988) According to Durkheim (1972), anomie results from a lack of strong ties, and the regulation and integration that they bring. This double source of constraints is seen as positive for the individual if they are balanced with clear benefits, and can help the individual's health compared to a system of no or loose ties (Segre, 2004). Durkheim therefore sees regulation as a positive, but nevertheless sees a potential danger of over-regulation (something which certainly seems applicable to education in national contexts such as England. Over-regulation doesn't lead to anomie, but to fatalism, which is the incapacity to internalise an unacceptable norm; because it is seen as unfair, or simply because it has been externally imposed or is excessively repressive (Besnard, 1988). Being part of networks is a key way of combating anomie, both thanks to the regulation that a social network brings, and the shared values that undergird this. Of course, anomie doesn't normally lead to suicide! However, it is linked to a range of other negative outcomes, one study for example finding that a low degree of anomie was related to high psychological quality of life and few psychosomatic symptoms on the one hand, and to good social integration and emotional support, a low amount of daily hassles and high educational level on the other hand, while high levels of anomie were related to high levels of psychosomatic symptoms and, therefore, greater demand for health interventions (Freidl, 1997).

There is empirical evidence to support the view that anomie is lessened where individuals have strong networks. Putnam (1995) reviews evidence that civic engagement is linked to participation in networks, and that strong network participation results in more positive outcomes in health and education. Putnam finds that decreasing membership of organisations and formal networks is linked to decreases in mutual trust between citizens. Similarly, Brashears (2010) finds that membership of a religious organisation and networking with others of like religious beliefs reduces anomie and personal unhappiness. A study on the relationship between poverty and health found that social ties could alleviate the negative impact of poverty on health outcomes, though it could not totally break the tie between poverty and ill health (Cattell, 2001).

This concept can be usefully applied to schools facing challenging circumstances, which may find themselves in situations of considerable stress and change with few links or ties to either other schools or the community, while often struggling to balance values of inclusiveness and social justice with the demands of performativity and competition that are foisted upon them. Networking in this sense may therefore not merely be important for school improvement in the traditional sense, but may impact positively on alleviating organisational anomie through providing integration and regulation with partner schools that may share the values and goals of schools facing challenging circumstances. Failing schools may often show strong signs of the anomie described by Durkheim, and their involvement in collaboration may show elements of a wish for increased regulation and integration. This may be seen in a willingness of such schools to take part in networks even as an unequal partner, supported by perceived stronger schools.

Durkheimian network theory also links to education in its focus on one issue that does not feature strongly in theories prevalent in the business field: moral purpose. Educational research and theory are increasingly positing moral purpose as a key factor in the successful performance of educational organisations (Harris & Lambert, 2003). Durkheim, in his theories of networking, sees moral purpose as playing a similarly important role, in that 'moral density', the taking into account of impact on society of the work of individuals, is seen as key to avoiding anomie (Segre, 2004). This ties in with the views of many school improvers, who posit that effective leaders in education have a strong moral purpose, that can enthuse and permeate the organisation and drive improvement and commitment of staff (Sergiovanni, 1999). We will discuss this further in the section on network density.

This theory would therefore appear to apply to collaborations and networks in which at least part of the motivation for collaboration is based on shared values and moral purpose, often with a strong equity perspective, rather than on more instrumental goals as predicted by social capital theory.

4.3 Functionalist Theories of Networking

A sociological theory which has had a great deal of influence in the past century is functionalism. Functionalism developed in the 19th century, and was strongly influenced by biological conceptions of society. Society was seen as a kind of organism that was characterised by gradual evolutionary development rather than radical revolutionary change. Of particular importance to functionalist views of society is the relationship between the elements of society and society itself, or between the parts and the whole constituted by them, particularly to functions which have to be fulfilled by the parts for the working of the whole. The parts are institutions such as forms of family life, economic production, government and religion as well as the organisational embodiments of such institutions: families, enterprises, governmental bodies, and churches. The institutions are binding rules which regulate the activities and relationships between people. The functions are, for example, biological reproduction for the family, generating resources and allocating them to needs for economic production, binding decisions for the collectivity for the government or the production of meaning for religion. One of the early functionalist sociologists was Durkheim, who we encountered earlier in this chapter. The basis of functionalism is that each social entity or function fulfils a role for society or individuals, and that this is why they come into being and persist. There are different schools within functionalism, and some schools take a weaker perspective that sees the function of entities within society, and indeed society itself, as hypotheses that need to be demonstrated in each individual case rather than as givens. The key methodology that was developed in this field was structural functionalism. In structural functionalism, the key goals were to discover what functions have to be fulfilled in order to secure the survival of society. Alongside this, functionalist researchers seek to find out what structures exist that enable these functions to be performed (Munch, 2001). Obviously education fulfils a number of important societal functions, such as social stratification (seen as a necessity to society in some functionalist theories), developing human capital to allow economic growth and competitiveness, and to develop personal wellbeing. Educational institutions such as schools will then evolve to best fulfil these functions. Functionalism is also common in the study of business organisations, and collaborative and networks in business. For example, Walter, Ritter, and Gemunde (2001) looked at the functions of business relationships and identified profit functions (profitable customer relations), volume functions (the need to sell a particular quantity of products in order to optimally utilise capacity and create economies of scale), and safeguard functions that maintain relationships with particular strong customers to provide a safeguard during periods of crisis or economic difficulty as direct functions of business relationships. Indirect functions capture connected effects in the future and/or in other relationships and the businesses wider network. They include innovation development, the scout function, in which businesses need to gain external information, and the access function, access to, for example, policymakers or credit. It is especially in these indirect functions that the role of networks may come to the fore.

A particularly important variant for us looking at networks is Luhmann's (1997) theory on the development of complex systems. Luhmann hypothesises that the reason complex systems evolve is because of the need for humans to reduce complexity they face in the environment. Once they exist, these systems, according to Luhmann, become self-referential or autopoetic. This means that to reduce complexity they become essentially concerned with creating and maintaining boundaries between themselves and the external world. However, while these autopoetic systems are constantly engaged in making and defining their boundaries, they are nevertheless open to external influence and complexity. External complexity is processed by the system which reacts to it in different ways. Systems maintain and develop largely through communication using an agreed and shared set of concepts and vocabularies, and external complexity is processed through the filter of this communication system.

In terms of the creation of networks functionalist theories will see these as primarily a means of fulfilling particular functions that would be harder for individual organisations. Networks will come into being when competitive pressures, lack of resources or complexity mean that a network is better able to fulfil the goals and needs of actors and society than a single entity.

The relevance of functionalist theories to networking in education is mainly situated at two levels. Firstly, a functionalist analysis of school networks will focus on reasons why networks are currently developing in education, i.e. in what ways might they be more effective in exercising the functions of schools in society. Alongside this, functionalist perspectives would study the most effective functional configuration of networks, and those factors that would make them more or less successful. This focus is clearly in some contrast with the new social movements approach, that focuses much more strongly on the role of individual actors and values in the development of networks. Secondly, Luhmann's theories of the development of self-referential systems are important. As we have mentioned earlier on in this book, educational environments are characterised by increasing complexity, especially for schools serving disadvantaged communities, where complex and diverse populations and needs are present, and multiple demands of accountability, parents and equity jostle for position. Added to this increased societal expectations of schooling and increased financial constraints and one can easily see situations developing where schools will form networks (which can be conceived as a move towards systemicity) to more easily confront this complexity. Furthermore, the need to define boundaries is clear when we start looking at the empirical evidence of networks engaged in efforts to create meaning, fight for power against other educational actors such as school districts, as is the importance of communication in the maintenance of networks. Where this functionalist view is weaker is the sense it creates that networks arise almost organically and naturally as a result of external conditions or needs (and this is a critique of functionalist thinking more generally). This obviously underestimates the extent to which networks do arise as the thoughtful actions of individuals rather than out of a systemic necessity.

A theory that is in many ways the opposite of functionalism, but that also has some relevance to networking is complexity theory. Which sees complex systems as made up of a large number of parts that show complex interactions. Such systems are hard to predict, as relationships are non-linear, as inputs and outputs relate non-linearly to one another due to unpredictable feedback loops. In this sense, complex causes can lead to simple outcomes and vice versa (Anderson, 1999). If we consider networks to be complex systems, which seems realistic in view of the complexity of ties and relationships that can exist within them, especially in the education sector where schools will typically be a part of multiple networks with multiple goals and actors, we can partially explain the sometimes differential outcomes of network activity, where we have seen a lot of variance in terms of effectiveness, results, and outcomes, in terms of results as well as relationships.

4.4 Conclusion

In these last two chapters, we have explored theoretical perspectives on networking and collaboration. We have described these as belonging primarily to an approach that takes a localised view of networks, or to an approach that takes a more societal view of networks and collaboration. Under the first approach I have included constructivist organisational theories, social capital theories and social network theories. Under the second, new social movement theory, Durkheimian notions of anomie and functionalist theories. Obviously this distinction is somewhat arbitrary, and you will have noticed some overlap between some of the theories discussed. Nevertheless, they each do shed a different light on networking and collaboration.

Interestingly, they also share two major similarities: none of them appears in itself to be sufficient to fully explain the phenomenon of networking between organisations, and none appears to be widely used as a framework for understanding collaboration and networking in education. This is unfortunate, as it is clear from the above that they can usefully inform both empirical and practical work and provide a clearer insight into ongoing processes and concerns.

Now that we have identified the key theoretical perspectives, we will look at creating typologies of networks and collaboratives in education.

Chapter 5
Towards a Typology of Educational Networks

Based on both theory and research, we will present a typology of educational networks differentiating them by factors such as network density, goals and purposes, and longevity. The typology is based on theoretical considerations and prior research, and will, along with the theories discussed in Chapters 3 and 4 provide a framework for discussing the case studies later on.

In the light of the growth of networks and the support for networking and collaboration as a school improvement strategy, an important question that needs to be answered is what the theoretical basis for networking is. In other words, why should organisations (and in particular schools) network, and what benefits should, theoretically at least, accrue from this?

5.1 Goals and Activities

The first dimension on which networks can be distinguished is that of goals and activities.

In contrast to views of networking as being necessarily concerned with learning and school improvement, other goals are both theoretically possible and present in the education system. For example, a renewed emphasis on full service schools and multiagency working has in many countries led to schools collaborating with each other and with external agencies to be able to provide a full service to pupils, addressing the social, health, and psychological needs of pupils in ways that would not be possible for individual schools (Sailor, 2002). Schools can also network, in the way businesses often do, to save material and staff costs, and to apply for funding through joint bids (Nooteboom, 2004); or for the provision of more effective and scalable CPD activities (Hadfield, 2005). It is clear that a pure school improvement orientation may therefore be too limited a viewpoint when discussing networking in schools. Therefore, network goals as they currently appear to exist in practice can be broadly defined as being about

- School improvement
- Broadening opportunities (including networking with non-school agencies such as social services or business)
- Resource sharing

D. Muijs et al., *Collaboration and Networking in Education*,
DOI 10.1007/978-94-007-0283-7_5, © Springer Science+Business Media B.V. 2011

As well as having different goals, school networks can be distinguished in terms of the timescale of activities undertaken. Activities undertaken by networks are obviously highly varied. Nevertheless, some key distinctions have been observed in terms of activity timescales. Some network activities are essentially short-term 'fixes', aimed at immediate issues of concern (such as getting out of special measures), but with little or no potential for longer-term impact. Others are intended to bring about much more fundamental changes (for example, changes in the school's culture or image), which may take several years to achieve, or lead to noticeable impacts. Many strategies fall somewhere in between (for example, a co-ordinated local strategy for inclusion, or setting up an action-learning set for head teachers), offering some combination of short-term impact and longer-term development.

Therefore, networking can be aligned along two dimensions, in terms of goals and activities, in the following way (Table 5.1):

Table 5.1 Goals and activities of networks with examples in each cell, taken from the authors' research

	Activities		
Goals	Short term	Medium term	Long term
School improvement	Partner school shares system to target D/C borderline pupils	School leaders support each other by sharing data and openly discussing approaches to school development. Leaders are available for support when necessary	Schools develop joint accountability systems, collegial leadership approaches and sustained support networks that draw in any new leaders in the network
Broadening opportunities	Partner schools put on a joint exam preparation day	Partner schools develop some shared courses, offering specific vocational courses in each partner school to all pupils in the partnership	Partner schools develop joint curriculum planning system, with development done collaboratively
Sharing resources	Teacher brought in from other school for Ofsted inspection	Teachers regularly help out in other network schools, with swapping and peer teaching common	Joint appointments made to the network, schools collaboratively plan recruitment and succession

Examples of each of these can be readily found in ongoing research on networking (e.g. West et al., 2006), and one example has been included in each cell. These examples are obviously far from exhaustive, and are offered as a snapshot rather than a definitive categorisation of all networking activities that may take place in schools.

They are also not intended to be normative. In particular, we do not intend to suggest that short-term activities are inherently less valuable than long-term activities. Dependent on the goals of the collaborative activities (e.g. coming out of special measures), the opposite may be true.

We can also link goals and activities to some of the theoretical approaches we discussed in the previous chapters, and networks may be classified on this basis. The following tables provide some examples, though need to be treated tentatively, as it is clear that some activities, for example, could be classified in more than one way depending on underlying purposes (Tables 5.2 and 5.3).

Table 5.2 Goals and theories

	Goals		
Theories	School improvement	Broadening opportunities	Sharing resources
Constructivism	Learning communities developed around joint subject groups	Schools work with local businesses and agencies to develop a better understanding of how to jointly address the needs of the local community	Schools put in place joint professional development programmes, where all schools in the network share the development of training resources
Social capital	Schools develop a supportive leadership network, where heads share their different areas of expertise in finance, marketing, and learning	Schools collaborate in curriculum provision by using the resources (e.g. industrial kitchen) in one school for courses across the network	Schools collaborate in hiring external consultants and developers for joint CPD events
New social movements	Schools come together to develop their own school improvement services outwith the LEA under the auspices of an activist head	Schools decide to form a network with local businesses and schools from another LEA to develop new curricular offerings	Schools join to lobby the LEA for additional resources under the leadership of the new head of one of the local schools
Durkheimian network theory	Schools serving a disadvantaged community form a network to develop shared working so staff can gain mutual support	Schools suffering falling roles develop joint curriculum in order to avoid closing provision seen as valuable to the community but with less student numbers in any one school	Schools decide to collaborate with the local church to share the church hall to develop parental outreach outside a school environment

Table 5.3 Activities and theories

	Activities		
Theories	Short term	Medium term	Long term
Constructivism	Schools engage in a joint problem-solving day around low performance in maths	Subject teachers regularly engage in joint CPD	Joint subject groups operating at the network level
Social capital	A curriculum expert from one school helps others develop a new timetable for the academic year	Schools can draw on one another's expertise in different subjects, by swapping teachers and occasionally using each others' resources	Schools in the network specialise in different areas and subjects
New social movements	Schools collaborate to lobby their LEA around a common problem	Schools decide to pool resources and develop their own CPD support	Schools develop a network that takes over most of the traditional roles of the LEA
Durkheimian network theory	Two schools threatened with special measures decide to hold common development day on preparing for LEA inspection	Schools facing challenging circumstances bring in an external consultant to develop a joint programme aimed at raising low literacy levels	Two schools facing challenging circumstances form a federation to pool resources and build capacity

5.2 What Networks? Further Classifications on Key Dimensions

As well as these theoretical distinctions, networks can be varied in form and can be categorised along a number of other key dimensions.

5.2.1 Voluntarism or Coercion

One dimension is the extent to which collaboration has been entered into voluntarily or, for at least one partner, under some form of coercion.

At one theoretical end of this continuum, one could find completely voluntary arrangements, whereby two or more schools form a network without any form of incentive. In practice this type of network will be rare, or be too informal to be the subject of mapping or research. At the other end of the continuum, we find networks in which two or more schools have been compelled to collaborate with one another by the government or Local Education Authority, for example with one school charged with improving the other. Again, in the English policy context of school-based management this arrangement will not usually occur in its pure form, though arrangements that are more or less coercive for at least one of the partners (for example the 'weak schools' in some two school federations) do exist. Most English examples of collaboration sit somewhere in between these extremes, with certain 'hard' federations tending towards the coercion continuum, while the Leadership Incentive Grants, for example, have led to a number of voluntary groupings, albeit with a financial incentive to collaborate.

Compulsion may, in some cases, be necessary to lead schools to improve, and has the advantage of greater control and opportunities for integration. It has clear disadvantages in terms of a likely reluctance of some members of staff in the school to fully engage in the network, and in the lack of trust that may result from this.

Below, we have given three examples of voluntary, intermediate, and coercive collaboration. Obviously, as mentioned this classification is a continuum, with many shades of networking in between the two poles (Table 5.4).

Table 5.4 Voluntary, intermediate, and coercive collaborations

Voluntary	Intermediate	Coercive
Schools voluntarily come together to form a network designed to take over some of the functions of a failing LEA	A government grant for collaborative activity leads the LEA to encourage schools to form a network	DfES informs a failing school that it will either have to Federate with a successful local school or close

5.2.2 Power Relations

An important dimension linked to the extent of coercion but not equal to it, is the extent to which relationships between networks are based on equality or on domination by one or more network partners. In theory, relations based on voluntarism should not be dominated by any actor, with partners working together to solve solutions on an equal basis (though issues of personal power, unequal status between partners or even unequal leadership capacities may modify this considerably), while coercive relations may be less so (although one can imagine coerced equal relationships, this is not a likely pattern).

Unequal relationships will frequently occur where a 'strong' school is paired with one or more 'weaker' schools to help these improve, a popular school improvement model in many Local Authorities in England (Lindsay et al., 2005). The advantage of the weak/strong school model can lie in the modelling and sharing of good practice from the 'strong' school to the weaker one (Chapman & Allen, 2005), though resentment and lack of cooperation among staff frequently result, with staff in the 'weak' school feeling that their strengths are not recognised and that they are being colonised by the stronger partner, while staff members in the stronger school can often be left wondering what the advantages of the collaboration with its increased workload are for them. On the other hand, a risk with voluntarism is the 'fat boy in the playground' syndrome, whereby certain schools will end up being seen as unattractive partners for networks, often those that could most benefit from them (Lindsay et al., 2005). While in theory the moral purpose of serving the community may compel head teachers to work with such schools anyway, enlightened self-interest within a competitive and performative framework may in many cases militate against this. Networks consisting of only weak school, however, often lack capacity collaboratively as much as the schools in the network do individually. Limited evidence suggests that collaborations may be more effective, at least in terms of getting off to a quick start, if they are either truly voluntary or coercive, while attempts to externally engineer communities of practice may be hard to get going (though this says nothing about long-term effectiveness) (Lindsay et al., 2005). Incentives to collaborate appear essential within a competitive culture that can otherwise make this problematic (Ainscow & West, 2005; Table 5.5).

Table 5.5 Voluntarism

Equal	Intermediate	Domination
Two neighbouring high-performing schools form a voluntary network to develop shared courses	A popular, high-performing school and a number of less high-performing schools form a network under the auspices of the LEA. While each school retains its head and autonomy, the perceived higher effectiveness of the first school gives that school more clout with the LEA and thus more influence in the network	A highly effective school is asked to take over a failing school through a federation. The head of the effective school becomes the head of the federation

5.2.3 Network Density

Networks can differ substantially with regard to their density. One way in which this can manifest itself is in the differential involvement of different groups in the process. As such, collaboration within the network can be largely a matter of heads and senior management, with little involvement (and in some cases little knowledge) of other staff groups (Muijs, 2006a). On the other hand, collaboration could involve specific groups of school staff, such as Science departments across schools, with agreement of senior managers but little actual involvement of members of the SMT. Theoretically, all staff could be involved through exchanges, visits, and joint meetings, though in practice this is unusual. Maximum density exists where everyone is connected to everyone else.

The extent to which pupils are directly impacted by collaborative activities within the network can similarly vary, from a direct impact through pupil and teacher exchanges or lessons followed in other network schools, through indirect impact resulting from good practice developed in network activity influencing classroom practice, to no impact on or involvement by pupils at all.

We can therefore see density as another continuum, where involvement can be mapped out by both number and seniority of staff involved. As we will discuss below for density of schools in a network higher density is not always desirable due to the increased complexity it entails. There may also be an element of redundancy in having too many contacts, and an element of confusion may occur as a result (Nooteboom, 2004). Some commentators, however, have described redundancy as a necessary correlate of effective networking as the complexity thereof could otherwise lead to the possibility of breakages in the network(s), and research from the Health sector suggests that greater density is associated with more beneficial outcomes, especially where complex outcomes need to be delivered, as can certainly be said to be the case of education (Hadfield, 2005, Nylen, 2007). A minimum level of density does appear essential to impact though, as involvement of very few people in an organisation is unlikely to have whole-school impacts.

Another perspective on density, depth of involvement, can be mapped out according to frequency of involvement, i.e. how many contacts are there, and depth of contacts, i.e. do contacts consists purely of meetings, or are there joint activities in terms of professional development, teacher exchanges, etc. At the extreme, deep involvement could eventually take the form of a merger between schools as happens in the private sector, although the problem of creating large, impersonal schools which are often seen as less effective than smaller schools is one that needs to be taken into account before going down this route.

In the table below we give some examples of how networks can vary in terms of density of staff and pupil involvement in collaboration (Table 5.6).

Table 5.6 Network density

Low density	Medium density	High density
Head teachers of network schools regularly meet and collaborate, but other staff are not directly involved	As well as a senior management group, there are cross network groups of subject leaders, pastoral leaders and some cross network groups engaged in specific school improvement activities, such as a data group. Not all staff, especially classroom teachers, are involved in collaborative work with colleagues from other schools	There is a joint senior management group for the network, subject teachers form cross-school networks and regularly teach in each others' schools, and pupils are engaged in joint activities such as exam preparation with pupils from other schools

5.2.4 External Involvement

An important dimension of educational networks is the extent to which external organisations or partners are involved with the network. This is frequently the case, with many networks formed around multiagency work involving social and child service agencies, while school improvement partnerships frequently involve Local Education Authorities, universities, or external consultants. The extent of involvement of these external bodies can vary considerably, from a purely brokering role at the start of the relationship to being an integral part of the relationship as is the case for partnerships between child service agencies and schools. In some cases the external partner can even be the main driving force behind the network, as is the case with some school reform programmes. It is, of course, entirely possible for networks to exist without external involvement, though in practice some form of brokering will typically have taken place. Community involvement can likewise vary considerably between networks, from none at all in many cases, to the community being an equal partner in the arrangement (though this is rare in practice) (Table 5.7).

Table 5.7 External involvement

Low external involvement	Medium external involvement	High external involvement
Schools have formed a voluntary network with minimal involvement of the LEA and no involvement of other external groups	Schools have formed a network under the auspices of the LEA. An LEA advisor is network coordinator, though this is largely a brokering and administrative role. The network also works with consultants from the local HEI	A charitable trust has invited schools to join in a network led by charity staff, who provide leadership, a full range of advisory services, resources, and data management

5.2.5 Different Time Frames

Collaborations can also have starkly differing time frames. Some collaborative arrangements can be intended to be more or less permanent and aimed at fundamental change, as is the case in the 'hard' federations, which are in many ways similar to merger arrangements in the private sector, while others can be very time-delimited, such as collaborations around a specific bid or initiative (Ainscow & West, 2005). There are of course a range of shades between these extremes, as well as some fluidity as initially short-term collaborations may grow into more permanent and lasting links.

In many cases there is no clarity on the intended duration of the collaboration. This is problematic (as we will see below), as it is not always desirable to maintain collaborations indefinitely because the same myopia that afflicts single organisation may end up affecting longstanding networks as well, and severing the link may be a more painful and difficult process where no prior end-point has been built in. However, there is some evidence from research that stability benefits network performance (Milward & Provan, 2003; Table 5.8).

5.2.6 Geographical Spread

A lot of the educational literature tends to assume that networking is largely a local affair, situated within local clusters or, at the outset, one local authority. Again, this is

Table 5.8 Different time frames

Short term	Medium term	Long term
Schools form a network to prepare for the closure of one of four schools in the locality. Once the closure has come into effect, the network will cease	Schools form a networked learning community working around distributed leadership. Once funding stops, schools intend to continue some form of collaboration, though this is very much a function of the enthusiasm of current leaders and may well cease once the head of one of the schools leaves	Schools form a federation with a joint governing body and joint executive head. Plans to locate all three schools on a shared site are at an advanced stage

but one possible form of networking, as cross-local, regional, and even international networks may and ever more frequently do occur as technological advances make this type of networking ever easier. While local networks may have the advantage of being set up to tackle specific local problems through a collaborative approach, they are often set up for purely practical reasons, such as existing LA links. In many cases a compromise is sought between the practical ease given by proximity, and lack of competition that is enabled by schools not serving the same catchments area, leading to networks across different areas of an LEA. Cross-regional networks are more frequently based on shared values or belief systems, and may in this respect be more coherent (Hadfield, 2005). Differences in intake, and a lack of support for specific local issues may be problems here, however.

A very specific form of cross-local networking is the franchise model, whereby schools collectively deliver a particular branded curriculum model. Private organisations are currently developing such franchised models (e.g. GEMS), but the extent to which these can count as instances of networks is doubtful in view of the strong central management involved, notwithstanding the links between schools in these models.

As well as varying in terms of their geographical reach, networks can also vary in terms of the extent to which they are cross-phase or not. Some extent of cross-phase collaboration has existed for a long time in education through the feeder school relationship between primary and secondary schools. Most extant collaborations and networks tend to focus on one phase however, with few going beyond the feeder school relationship as far as cross phase networking goes (Table 5.9).

Table 5.9 Geographical spread

Proximity	Medium distance	High distance
Two neighbouring schools serving a disadvantaged area form a federation	Schools network with schools in a neighbouring LEA, forming a regional network	A group of schools across the country run by the Jesuit order form a network on the basis of shared values

5.2.7 *Density of Schools*

Networks also differ in terms of the number of schools involved. Interestingly, a lot of the theory of networks seems to refer to dyadic relationships, even though these are by no means the most prevalent in practice (Nooteboom, 2004). It is clear that networks can differ substantially in size, and can also expand and contract over time. Contraction usually occurs when certain network members become disengaged from the network and drop out, a particular problem in larger networks where a small core often ends up driving the activities. Scaling up can be problematic, as it represents a fundamental change in the relationship between partners, especially when scale up happens from a low base, as in a change from a dyadic to a triadic network (Simmel, 1950).

Within large networks, density of collaboration can differ in terms of the number of connections between schools within the network. Again, maximum density occurs where all schools are connected to one another. It has to be pointed out here that while high density may appear desirable in terms of deepening the collaboration and maximising opportunities for collaborative learning and cultural change, overly dense collaboration can be problematic, due to the increased complexity of managing them. Indeed, given that the maximum number of direct connections is $n(n-1)/2$, the complexity of the network rises with the square of the number of participants (Nooteboom, 2004). There is therefore a balance that needs to be struck between the desirability of high levels of connectivity and the increased complexity of managing these. Once networks become large, a centre-periphery model tends to emerge, where certain organisations form a core driving the network, while others are more peripherally connected to it. Coordination becomes ever more important, and centrality of the organisation in the network starts taking on a greater significance as it leads to power and control of the information flow. Density is not a requirement for the development of social capital, as weaker ties can also be effective as long as they plug the structural holes in actors' knowledge and skills.

According to Lin (1999), dense ties are more effective for preserving and maintaining resources as a denser network allows more chance of mobilising many others to help defend the threatened resource, while more flexible and weaker links may be more effective for obtaining new resources. While multiple partnerships may be desirable, a surfeit of networks may be problematic for schools in that it can hinder clarity and purpose (Lindsay et al., 2005). No relationship between density and impact was found in the CUREE (2005) systematic review.

Durkheim (1972) makes an interesting distinction between material density, which can be characterised as similar to the concept of density presented here, and moral density, which he characterised as occurring when social actors doing their specialised work interact with and take into account their collaborators, while being aware of the consequences of their actions for society as a whole.

In practice, the smallest networks obviously consist of two schools, while the largest networks, we are aware of, contain not more than 15 schools, though larger networks are theoretically possible. An intermediate network would then consist of between five and ten schools.

5.2.8 *Vertical or Horizontal Networking*

A final distinction that can be made is related to the extent to which collaboration is vertical, i.e. within schools, as opposed to horizontal, i.e. between schools. This is again a continuum, whereby schools can be situated along two poles in terms of vertical collaboration (as mentioned in the section on depth of networks), but can likewise be situated along two poles in terms of the extent to which this vertical networking goes along with internal networking in the school. This can be near to non-existent, can be at the individual teacher level, and can operate within departments, or, in the case of the most 'collaborative' schools, across departments. As with vertical networking, the number of people involved and the extent of interaction can be differentiated. Thus, schools can be mapped along depth of networking vertically and horizontally, potentially providing a useful heuristic tool allowing us to probe more closely the relationship between (extent of) networking and organisational performance. Some examples are given below (Table 5.10):

Table 5.10 Horizontal or vertical networking

Vertical networking	Horizontal networking	Horizontal and vertical networking
Joint working groups exist within the school around specific school improvement priorities, such as data management and literacy, but there is no external networking	Subject heads from schools within a network have working groups around their subjects, but no such mechanisms exist internally in the school	Joint working groups exist within the school around specific school improvement priorities, and one representative of each within school group sits on a cross school network committee around the same priority

Obviously networks will be classifiable along different dimensions, such that we could describe a network as voluntary, medium density, intermediately dominated, and with high external involvement, for example.

5.2.9 *Network Diffuseness*

Networks can also be more or less diffuse, in the sense that they may be composed of a loose collection of actors, shifting in membership (such as would be the case in a situation where a group of local schools sets up informal meetings or problem-solving working parties around specific issues) or, at the other extreme, be a fixed, finite groups of actors that are connected in formal mechanisms. Rather than diffuse in this case the network is formed of exclusive relationships (this would be the case in a 'hard federation' of schools, connected by a joint governing body, for example) (Uzzi, 1996). No one form of network has been found to be most effective, rather, networks appear to be more effective if they don't have a form imposed upon them, though it appears that accountability of the network to a higher power encourages actors to develop optimal network structures (Milward & Provan, 2003).

5.2.10 Network Formalisation

In terms of the management of networks, and the relationship between actors in the network, networks can be characterised as being more or less formalised. In some cases networks rely largely on trust and good faith, and require little in the way of formalised agreements or management structures. This type of network can be highly effective in that problems can be easily and flexibly resolved. However, they can be strongly reliant on relations between individuals and can run into difficulties where staff changes occur. There can also be difficulties when things go wrong, where it can be unclear where responsibility for service provision lies and therefore who is ultimately accountable. In more formalised arrangement contracts, management structures and formal agreements can attenuate these problems, but can also limit flexibility and responsiveness, and can in some cases militate against the development of trusting relationships. Moving from informal to formal collaboration can be disruptive to existing relationships (Nylen, 2007). In its most extreme manifestation formalisation can lead to the setting up of specialised units or structures specifically charged with organising the collaboration, which obviously entails significant costs. The evidence suggests that the greater the cultural distance between organisations and the less they have previously worked together the greater the need for formalisation.

5.3 Conclusion

There are therefore a range of dimensions along which we can classify networks, and which all have consequences in terms of the choices that need to be made when engaging in networks, as they may carry different costs, levels of complexity, and potential rewards. The situation is further complicated by the fact that these dimensions interact with one another. For example, there is evidence that there is a relationship between network density and formalisation in that higher levels of density appear to require lower levels of formalisation. In highly complex situations, on the other hand, both high levels of formalisations and high levels of density may be required, as where different organisations have to combine to deliver services to groups with complex needs, as may be the case with a collaboration between special schools (Nylen, 2007).

Part II
Networking in Practise

Chapter 6
Federations of Schools: Case Studies of Practice

6.1 Introduction

The launch of the federations policy in England signalled a new phase of policy development in the move towards encouraging collaboration (see Chapter 1). While federal structures do exist in other countries, including the Netherlands, for the first time in England collaboration between schools had the potential to be more than individuals and teams working across organisational boundaries the 2002 Education Act made it possible for governing bodies to change organisations structural configurations to support school-to-school collaboration.

In 2007 the federations policy was reinforced through central to the English government's 'Transforming Secondary Education' agenda. Within this agenda, diversity and collaboration were the two main driving forces for raising standards and improving teaching and learning. Federations are viewed as an innovative strategy for improving schools in challenging circumstances and for confronting underperformance and school failure. Federations are supposed to provide increased opportunities for sharing staff and other resources, joint professional development, curriculum development, leadership, and management. It is also argued that a federation can extend curriculum opportunities for young people at 14–19 level and promote inclusion in the broadest sense. Each federation is configured to meet local conditions and can therefore be responsive to the particular educational challenges its community faces.

In terms of definition, the term 'federation' has been broadly interpreted and applied. It has been used to describe many different types of collaborative groups, partnerships, and clusters, even through to mergers and the creation of new schools. For the purposes of this study, federations were defined in two ways:

- The definition as invoked in the 2002 Education Act which allows for the creation of a single governing body or a joint governing body committee across two or more schools from September 2003 onwards.
- A group of schools with a formal (i.e. written) agreement to work together to raise standards, promote inclusion, find new ways of approaching teaching and learning and build capacity between schools in a coherent manner. This will be brought about in part through structural changes in leadership and management, in many

D. Muijs et al., *Collaboration and Networking in Education*,
DOI 10.1007/978-94-007-0283-7_6, © Springer Science+Business Media B.V. 2011

instances through making use of the joint governance arrangements invoked in the 2002 Education Act.

The former have been termed 'hard' federations as they are tightly coupled sitting at the more formal end of the spectrum of collaborative arrangements. Across all types of federations, whether 'hard' or 'soft', it is generally recognised that there is a need for high levels of trust, co-operation, and confidence. Consequently, while the government has been keen to promote all forms of school-to-school collaboration it is arguable that groups of schools need to take a measured and staged approach to partnership to guarantee impact and success.

This chapter focuses on the issues related to governance and leadership in federations. It is structured in four sections. The Introduction has outlined the educational context and provided a definition of terms. The second section of this paper provides an overview of the methods used to collect and analyse the case study data. The third section highlights the key themes emerging from the data. The Conclusion discusses the findings and argues the development of a more federated system may provide an opportunity for developing more context-specific approaches to improving schools facing challenging circumstances.

6.2 Methods

This study aimed to investigate and highlight the relative benefits and limitations of various forms of federation (i.e. 'hard' and 'soft'). The research was guided by a number of overarching research questions pertaining to governance, leadership, and management, including:

- What are the emerging forms of governance within federations of schools?
- What are the emerging forms of leadership and management within federations of schools?
- To what extent can federations support school improvement?

The case study data collected throughout the evaluation both illuminates and illustrates the potential and potency of collaboration between schools. It also shows the sheer diversity and range of activity occurring under the umbrella term of 'federations'. The two main elements of this study were case studies of a sample of the 37 federations in the programme together with surveys of schools in the non-case study federations. This paper focuses on the findings relating to governance, leadership and management from the case study strand of research.

6.2.1 Identification and Selection of Case Studies

Ten federations were selected as case studies using a sequence of criteria to ensure a sample that reflected the range within the project. Two of the original 10 federations declined to continue from Phase 2 of the study. A new federation was included in Phase 3. The final sample, therefore, comprised nine very varied case studies. Selection was made on the basis of maximum variation sampling drawing on DfES summaries of the federations derived from their original bids.

The first criterion was type of governance. This varied in terms of a 'soft-hard' continuum, reflecting increasing power and responsibility for a governance system for the federation. At the 'softer' end, federations comprised schools voluntarily joining together for specific purposes with relatively informal arrangements. Governing bodies of individual schools retained independent power. At the 'harder' end, schools set up new systems of governance which supported stronger links between schools. These could include joint meetings of governors, service level agreements approved by all governing bodies, and moves towards a single governing body for the federation.

The main second order criteria were the aims of the federation and the types of schools/organisations involved. Aims reflected governance. For example, federations developed on the model of a successful school supporting a school experiencing difficulties had, or were working towards, forms of governance where there were formal arrangements and structures. Where the focus was on continuing professional development, for example, governance appeared to be primarily based in the individual schools with informal arrangements between governing bodies. Sampling also ensured there was a range of sizes of federations (from 2 to 20) and of institutions. Consequently, some federations comprised only schools of a single phase, others crossed school phases, and others included Further Education (FE) colleges and/or other services. Finally, geographic spread was also taken into account to ensure both urban and rural locations and a distribution across England.

6.2.2 Data Collection and Analysis

Data collection was undertaken in three phases in order to gain information on the early stages of the federation, its mature phase and finally the phase at which DfES funding was coming to an end. Documents including original bids, Ofsted reports, governing body papers, and development/improvement plans were examined throughout the project. Over 100 interviews were conducted during each phase of the study with key participants, including:

- The federation 'lead', who was typically its director or chief executive, but could be a senior LA officer instrumental in developing the federations;
- Head teacher/college principals;
- Chairs of governors and members of governing bodies;
- Teachers holding posts of responsibility such as year tutor;
- Other professionals.

All interviews were semi-structured and followed proformas appropriate to the phase and interviewee. For example, Phase 1 interviews addressed setting up the federation, plans, and expectations, whereas Phase 2 focussed on the embedding process, and Phase 3 interviews included reflections on reasons for and barriers undermining success, sustainability and the interaction between the development of the federation and other government policies and initiatives over the period, including Every Child Matters, inclusion, Education Improvement Partnerships and the proposals for Trust schools. The study also included attendance at federation meetings.

All interviews were recorded and notes were taken during interviews. Researchers also made field notes during site visits to capture insights into relationships and events as they occurred in the field. Twenty-five percent of all interviews were fully transcribed. Marginal annotations were used to identify emerging themes patterns and trends within and between cases. Field notes and interview recordings from transcribed interviews also fed into this processes. After each round of visits an account of practice was constructed and fed back to the Federation for validation purposes. The accounts of practice were built up over time. These accounts formed the basis of case study reports for each federation (see Lindsay et al., 2005).

6.3 Findings

This section of the paper draws on the case study data to present key findings relating to the governance, leadership, and management of federations

6.3.1 Governance Arrangements

Underlying the concept of 'federation' is a different level of governance beyond schools simply making informal arrangements to collaborate in particular activities. Discussion of types of federation often used the 'hard-soft' continuum as one key variable. A 'hard' federation has a different governing body structure with powers removed from isolated constituent schools and invested in a new federation governing body. At the other end of the continuum ('soft') the governing bodies are unchanged and all activities are arranged by agreement.

In the case studies we found a continuum, not a dichotomy. Indeed, the defining characteristic, even in the early stages, was the lack of uniformity. Even within the 'hard' federation there appeared to be different models while in the middle of the continuum there are examples of varying degrees of changes to governance. In one example there was a Strategic Management Board (SMB) comprising two members of each school's governing body together with head teachers, the Federation Director and Assistant Director, and an LA representative. In another example, there was an interim Partnership Board including governors from each school and their head teachers, which was expected to give way to a Federation Board. At the 'soft' end, Federation G had neither Executive Head or Development Manager, nor any formal governing body spanning the schools.

6.3.1.1 Soft Federations

Federation D was essentially a collaborative proposal for the secondary and feeder primary schools, but in practice there was some tension, even suspicion, between the partners. Within the primary heads there was a feeling that federating may be a 'take over' attempt by the secondary school.

> There was quite a fear that there would be one governing body for all five schools and, you know are we looking at some type of superhead position where somebody is taking a controlling role in all five schools (primary head).

The primary schools were unclear as to whether 'soft' may progress to 'hard' and were uneasy about this. They were also unclear about the leadership, management, and legal roles and responsibilities and how this ambiguity might impact on their own school governance and autonomy. As the process developed, these fears reduced.

By the end of the study, variation in models of governance remained. While some federations continued to evolve, others continued unchanged. The secondary head of Federation D, dispelled the initial fears of the primary head teachers, reporting that: *There have been no real changes to governance as a result of the Federation.* In terms of governance this was a 'soft' federation. Each school has its own governing body; the federation however, has a joint governance/strategic committee without delegated powers. All schools within the federation shared a set of common goals that bind federation activity together. There were agreed protocols and the joint committee can make recommendations but it is up to individual governing bodies to authorise plans. There was no common budget and each school retained their DfES number. The Strategic committee decided how the DfES pump-priming federation grant was used over the 3 years of the project. In terms of staffing, there have been some joint appointments and movement of staff between schools. However, the federation has been unable to appoint a federation principal/manager despite offering an attractive salary and re-advertising the position. Therefore this role continues to be the preserve of the secondary school head teacher.

Federation F provides an example of how federation governance can evolve over a period of time. The basic structure of a SMB has continued—half way through the study the federation director reported that its meetings had been *real drivers for change and accountability*. Proposals to amend the constitution were under consideration by the four governing bodies as there was no significant budget for the SMB. The re-drafted constitution casts the SMB into a monitoring (rather than strategic) role and recommends that the terms of reference for a full governing body make it more explicit that the school-based governing bodies are to monitor their schools' contributions to the federation. The revised constitution also foresees a reduced number of SMB meetings (three times a year). A chair of governors did not think that the role of the governing bodies had developed over the life-time of the federation. While governors' responsibilities and statutory duties had increased substantially, their role had not really developed and the SMB meeting was simply another 'talking shop'.

Federation C took an alternative approach. Although there was no joint governing body for the federation, the federation decided to develop legal status by setting itself up as a limited company with a joint governing body. An executive group of head teachers became the board of the limited company and the governors meet as a scrutiny committee as members of the company, in order to get them involved, but without the binding legal power of a 'hard' federation. The choice of company status was generally seen as very successful. It has allowed the federation to appoint staff working specifically for the federation, such as the coordinator and an advisor. Human Resources policies have so far been somewhat unclear with regard to matters such as pension conditions, although this is changing now as more people are federation employed. Company status has also made it easier for the federation to enter into contracts with other organisations and to provide services. It gives the federation a sense of structure: *It is a statement of intent. It's like musketeers stepping into the ring and saying 'we really mean this'* (head, secondary school). Capacity for growth in the federation without external pressure is seen as a further advantage. According to the chair of governors of a large federation school, the fact that the federation is a company has led to a stronger feeling of ownership among the schools. *If you want to make something work, make sure people have a financial interest in it.*

Both Federations A and B had shared governance committees but with limited authority. In Federation B the committee comprised governors from each school but with no statutory powers. In both cases the meetings of governors provided a forum for communication and discussion rather than decisions. In both cases, there was a strong commitment to respecting the individual ethos of schools, and indeed their governing bodies. In Federation A, joint governor training had developed which was now being taken up by the LA.

6.3.1.2 'Hard' Federations

Federation E, however, had proceeded from the earlier Partnership board to a Federated Governing Body of the three schools. This, the most radical development among the case studies, had experienced a number of challenges during its development. The original proposal for the federation had included bringing the three schools into one building but without an explicit plan to have only one school, although such a possibility was under consideration as a possible long-term option. In the absence of a definitive long-term policy several factors became apparent. Firstly, the process of developing the system had caused some difficulties in the early stages. As one interviewee noted, *I was absolutely astounded to learn that the first time the three governing bodies had come together was just over a month ago.* The changes of head teacher at the secondary school interacted as these resignations and appointments reflected different views by those in post compared with the LA's vision, but the change of key staff was disruptive, both because this had resulted in three different heads and because some secondary staff felt their voice was lessened.

Initially, the governors also had concerns. The discussion of a 'soft' or 'hard' federation was reported by one governor to be a 'sticking point' but in the end they had decided to *bite the bullet* and support the hard version. Governance was initially through a partnership board although there was a separate project board which guided the government backed Private Finance Initiative (PFI) building of the new school. The partnership board included three governors from each school and their head teachers. The Director of Education described the relationship between these as *The Partnership Board being the operational doer and the Project Board being the executive arm that would take key decisions if the Partnership Board were unable to take them.* The development of the model had not been easy, with both practical concerns (e.g. how many governors per school) and other matters particular to specific schools. The Director thought that, *if anybody wants to know how to do it, we can tell them how to do it, now, and based on our mistakes. But, you know, you never learn unless you make mistakes.*

In the early stages, the governing bodies were seen to be pulling in different directions at times. They were in a difficult position. As governors, they had a duty to consider the development of the federation, but they also took seriously their responsibility towards their own school. This caused tensions *I think everybody was pulling in their own direction, as it were, and it wasn't coming together* (secondary head). Each had its own culture and history and had different degrees of interest in and commitment to either federating or the importance of the inclusion agenda. There were also technical questions regarding the legal status of a joint body and the basis for representation for each school; would the secondary school, by nature of its size, have an inbuilt majority of governors?

Nevertheless, the governors were positive in principle, not least because they could see the benefits of the new building that came with the federation. They would have liked joint meetings of the governing bodies earlier in the planning stage but they had voted in favour of the federation and governors interviewed articulated benefits in terms of joint working and sharing expertise. However, these early positive perspectives were to some extent replaced by doubts as the realities of the federation became apparent, e.g. budget decisions.

The early days of the federated governing body required a substantial commitment from its members. A number of sub-committees were set up to which tasks were delegated. These were not organised around schools but themes, seen as an important decision. Another fundamental issue was the decision to pool all schools' budgets: *We couldn't do what we now do if we hadn't got that (single budget)* (executive director). Similarly, the workforce reform received *outright opposition from both (primary and secondary) schools until the new secondary head gave his support for (what he termed) this brilliant idea* (executive director). By the end of the study the federation was able to address economies of scale and there was support for the single budget.

The partnership board, set up initially, was replaced in April 2005 by the federated governing body which took over the responsibilities from the three separate governing bodies, which were disbanded. These two bodies had the benefit of committed and highly respected chairs who were able to steer the development of the federation during these challenging times with sensitivity and efficiency widely assisted by those in the committees. It was apparent also that by the summer of 2006 members of the Federated Governing Body generally had high regard for their colleagues. The difficulties and contentiousness of some issues were recognised but there was also appreciation of the positive contribution of governors:

> When the governing bodies were dissolved and we created the federated governing body, then it took on a whole new meaning and people were starting to look, particularly at that level, at the good of the federation
>
> (Member of federated governing body)

These examples provide a flavour of the range of governance models developed by federations. Most are towards the 'soft' end of the continuum with governance responsibility remaining primarily with the constituent schools. The joint bodies, with various titles, were set up to facilitate, provide fora for discussion and to provide opportunities for joint strategic planning but generally they had only limited decision-making powers. In this sense, Federation E provides a substantially different model, but one that was regarded as necessary given the nature of the federation. In some case studies, governance remained throughout the 'life' of the federation (e.g. Federation G) while others debated governance and amended slightly, rejecting a move towards harder-edged arrangements (e.g. Federation F) and others evolved (e.g. Federation L).

6.3.2 Leadership and Management

6.3.2.1 Context of Federation Leadership and Management

Federations differed in the extent to which they were developed from historical, collaborative working relationships. Those that involved successful schools joining with schools in difficulty were essentially collaborations engineered out of adversity with an in-built power and status differential, which in one case at least was quickly renegotiated by the schools involved. Federations that grew out of past collaborations, however, had a greater sense of equality. However, this description, while having general validity, is too simplistic. In the case studies we found other, more subtle variations.

Federation A grew out of a pre-existing local Head Teachers' Conference which itself was an outgrowth of other developments. As one head teacher put it, *The federation gives us the money to do what we were already doing*—speculating that the federation would not have achieved nearly so much had it started as a new initiative when the funding began. All of the head teachers interviewed placed importance on the trust between the heads themselves as the foundation of the network. This was echoed by a governor, who cited it as a positive influence which had allowed the federation to be much *further down the road* than it would have been otherwise. This was a 'soft' federation, in that there was no legal relationship between schools. The chair of the federation described himself as *primus inter pares*, and emphasised the need for independence among the schools. In spite of this 'soft' nature, however, head teachers within the federation were clear that the structures which were in place allowed for more consistent and useful work between the schools than a looser, more ad hoc relationship (such as was extant for other areas of the LA). A discordant voice was heard, however, from a head who had previous experience of a more tightly structured federation elsewhere, and felt that Federation A could be more effective if the structure were to be tightened.

This example indicates the benefits of pre-existing collaboration but it is necessary to note they are federations by agreement. These schools saw an opportunity to do more of what they were already doing, but better. Federation B, however, comprising two secondary schools, one of which was having difficulties, had a less equal relationship at the start. The two schools involved in the secondary network had not previously had much collaboration; therefore, there was a great deal of ground work to be done before the federation could be successful, as the head teachers themselves acknowledge. This was compounded by three other issues: the preconceptions staff had about what federation might be/entail; existing ways of working in one of the schools; and the local authority's (school district) original idea of what the federation should be. Before the federation got off the ground, there was a good deal of speculation in the national education press which head teachers are convinced was unhelpful. In essence, this information seems to had led staff to believe that all federations would be 'hard', would have joint governance, and led to staff fears of loss of school identity, of head teachers becoming remote, and of changes in employment status and conditions. As one of the head teachers pointed out,

> Because we were a softer federation it would have been much more helpful if we could have called ourselves a collaborative from day one . . . But it was very hard because forces from without—and I would include the LEA in that—were really quite locked into the idea of a hard federation—that was my perception anyway—hard in the sense of accountability and change
>
> (Head teacher)

This example also highlights the 'hard-soft' dimension. The schools saw themselves in a soft federation despite the focus on improving standards in one of the constituents, whereas others in this model developed harder types of governance systems with a formal agreement or contracts.

6.3.3 Senior Leadership and Management Within Federations

Federations differed in the use of an overall 'leader'. Terminology, function, and power also varied. In some cases there was a chief executive who saw their role as concerned with facilitation:

> My role has stayed the same. Although I'm the chief executive, my role is to be chief facilitator, to bring people together to discuss things.

In this instance, the chief executive was the head teacher of the secondary school in Federation D who had been instrumental in the setting up of the federation. The secondary school exhibits an entrepreneurial approach and was opportunistic in terms of developing materials and activities that could add value to the federation's work. This is an example of a 'loosely coupled' model where participants negotiate their level of involvement and nature of contribution.

Some federations introduced posts of director or chief executive. In the case of one federation that withdrew from the study the chief executive had been the head teacher of the successful secondary school. When he took on this chief executive post he was replaced as head by his deputy, a strategy also noted in a recent study of this model of federation (Glatter & Harvey, 2006). In Federation E, the LA had originally planned to appoint the head of the secondary school as chief executive but, when he resigned, they rethought and subsequently appointed the head of the special school as acting chief executive. Over the time, the federation 'hardened' and has moved towards a single school, with the acting chief executive having been confirmed as chief executive of the federation.

In other cases, a federation appointed a director who was not simultaneously a head teacher, but with a clear leadership role and appointed at a level to match this. Such directors had a delicate path to tread but were very successful. For example, in Federation H where the federation principal provides the strategic leadership. During the early stages of development of the federation, the principal paid particular attention to developing and communicating a vision for the federation based on the support for the failing schools (schools placed on Special Measures by the Office for Standards in Education (Ofsted)). This involved making key appointments and providing leadership capacity in key areas. Once Schools A and B had been removed from Special Measures much of the vision had been accomplished. Therefore the federation leadership revisited their core values and beliefs in an attempt to develop a shared vision for future development. The outcomes of these discussions will dictate how the federation will evolve and the nature of leadership roles and responsibilities assigned to individual leaders. This is a challenging task because tensions exist within the leadership group. The federation has created an additional tier of management. A governor highlighted how the new structure has impacted on the head teachers:

> When a head teacher has been directly responsible to his [*sic*] governors and now he's responsible to his Principal as well as his governors. I mean it's taking something away from his original authority (federation governor).

The head teachers also recognised their power and autonomy have been eroded. One reflected:

> You're not a head any longer; you are merely managing a department ... (federation head teacher)

In Federation E, head teachers left their posts over the period of the federation's planning and development, the last despite having an important role to play in moving towards a new management structure that abolished the roles of the head teachers other than the executive director.

The personal styles and commitment of the federation leaders were seen as very important to success, whatever the formal designation of the post of chief executive/director. The Partnership Director was seen as a vital part of the work of Federation I, described as

> A human dynamo. He's passionate about what we're doing and when there is a barrier... he'll find a way round it and to have that sort of leadership helps. ... [He]'s been the facilitator, the leader, the inspiration for us to move forward (head teacher).

Similar comments were made by other interviewees in this federation. Losing the project management and with it the drive to move things forward would spell the end of the federation, because head teachers are not able to do it. An assistant head pointed out that the head teachers all needed to support the federation for it to be maintained, with the Partnership Director the *real driving force*, adding that she would not want to lose the part of the federation with which she was involved.

The importance of these personal characteristics of drive and commitment, but coupled with sensitivity, was evident across the sample. Drive and similar characteristics have also been reported as likely key success factors when a successful school combines in some sense with a school in difficulties. However, sensitivity is less central in those cases. Indeed, the head charged with helping to turn the other school round may consider there are hard decisions to be made, and quickly, such as removing staff and pupils (Glatter & Harvey, 2006). In the current study, however, the majority of schools were federations of choice, so working relationships had to be developed not imposed. Many schools, while happy to collaborate, sought to maintain their autonomy. For example, in Federation A the need to maintain autonomy was articulated by the federation chair (who was also a head teacher), the administrator (a deputy head) and other heads and, although not expressed as such, this desire for autonomy might militate against there ever being a 'hard' federation with a chief executive who had power to intervene in constituent schools. While interviews in this federation's schools did not indicate a concern for autonomy in such trenchant terms, it was still apparent that individual cultures were considered sacrosanct. One head teacher spoke of consistency across the network in terms of issues such as ear and body piercing and uniforms and in terms of relationships with parents and pupils, but not in terms of conformity of pedagogy and structure.

6.3.4 Middle Level Leadership and Management in Federations: Ownership and Involvement

During Phase 1 of the study, middle managers, teachers, and governors had relatively little understanding of the federation of which they were part. This may suggest proposals to the DfES for funding as a federation had been created and owned by senior members of staff. This is perhaps not surprising. One reality for schools over recent years has been the importance of responding quickly to new government initiatives, especially those that brought resources into schools. This is not a cynical reaction but one developed out of necessity. Furthermore, as previously discussed, many of these federations were already committed to collaboration and partnership. Consequently, bids built upon existing practice but were typically developed without extensive discussions throughout the schools.

Over the period of the study, however, other staff and governors became more knowledgeable and enthusiastic and there were opportunities, for example, for middle managers to take on whole school and federation-wide roles. This was not always the case, although reasons could be complex. For example, in Federation A there was a marked difference in enthusiasm for the federation as one delved down: senior staff were generally quite enthusiastic; governors were supportive but unable to show much impact on the life of the school; some teachers were unenthusiastic at best. Two teachers could see no gains to be accrued from the federation or its work. Perhaps significantly, these teachers saw little input from the federation or any other network in terms of information and resources, that is, in terms of immediate impact on teaching rather than on any long term issues.

This may indicate that the federation concentrated on upper level issues—choice of specialism for federated schools seeking specialist status, fresh start, etc. rather than classroom based change. As head teachers were so enthusiastic about the work of the federation it may be the case that the federation served and supported their work. This does not mean, of course, that there was no effect in the classroom—in fact, it is clear that initiatives run through the federation had significant effect in the classroom. However, this work was not branded as federation led or inspired. This lack of branding was almost certainly linked to, if not a direct result of, the culture of independence and individual ethos mentioned above. Schools undertook initiatives which were supported by the federation but those initiatives remained school based and owned.

In other cases, the impact of the federation was readily appreciated and commented upon by the staff throughout the school and by governors. These instances were characterised by clear branding of initiatives as part of the developing federations, for example the emphasis on continuing professional development in Federations D, G, and I and the development of an initiative to promote inclusion in Federation I. The latter was developed over a period of the project and by May 2006 had been rated *good, with outstanding features* by Ofsted.

6.4 Conclusion

The findings from this study support the literature that suggests successful change is underpinned by ownership of the change residing with teachers (Fullan, 1991), and that all change is local (Datnow et al., 2002). Where the federations worked well and the schools were keen for their continuation it was clear they had addressed their own internally driven priorities in their own way. These were schools coming together with a common purpose rather than being forced into alliances to solve problems defined and driven by outside agencies. These initiatives could be built upon positive action, to enhance existing good practice, but there were also examples of schools working together to support one or more schools experiencing significant difficulties. However, in the latter case also, the schools developed a federation that was more collegial and equal than a simple 'good school—weak school' combination, with its implications of differential power and value.

The notion of interdependence is associated with successful collaboration particularly in urban and challenging contexts (Ainscow & West, 2006). This was found in the present study where schools in the more successful federations had developed strong interdependent relationships based on the assumption that all partners within the federation could learn from each other, rather than the relationships promoting a one way transfer of ideas, knowledge, and resources from the 'good' school to the 'weak' school. This was viewed as being important in avoiding a dependency culture where the weaker school is reduced to a 'performance training sect' holding negligible internal capacity (Hargreaves, A., 2003a).

Beyond issues of local ownership and control within a context of interdependence the findings reveal a greatly variegated picture. The nine case studies, in particular, have indicated there is a lack of conformity on all the major themes by which we have analysed the data. This is particularly evident when considering models of governance, leadership, and management.

6.4.1 Reflecting on Governance

Sullivan and Skelcher (2002) provide a helpful taxonomy of forms of collaboration and rules of governance within the public sector. They argue that the loosest form of collaboration involves informal networks underpinned by self-governance through mutual norms and obligations and shared values and trust. Within this continuum networks become defined as partnerships when parties agree to share a limited amount of information. Such partnerships become more formalised and move towards becoming a federation when there is agreement to undertake joint activity and constitute a formal governing body. However, it is argued that the defining feature of a federation is the creation of a *federal structure in which participating bodies agree to devolve upwards some of their autonomy* (p. 43), this is underpinned by external government through an overarching constitution. At the extreme, Sullivan and Skelcher describe the merger of participating bodies into a single organisation as integration. Federations in this study fell in most parts of this continuum, though none reached genuine integration.

Governors, especially chairs of governing bodies, were key to the setting up of the federation but thereafter the role of governing bodies was often relatively limited. This was the case more often with softer federations, where reports to individual governing bodies or relatively informal joint committees of governors were seen as more appropriate. Harder federations, however, needed to set up systems of governance. One federation moved through a partnership board to a federated governing body over the period of the study, as the nature of the federation took shape and responsibilities changed.

Central to the structure of governance was finance. In most federations schools retained their own budgets. The discussion regarding finance, therefore, was firstly to agree on the use of the DfES grant under this programme and secondly whether, and if so by how much, to pool resources, and what accountability measures could be put into place. The federation's approach to pooling resources was an important factor in its likely sustainability after the funding ceased. It was evident that loosening and giving up control of the school budget was a fundamental issue for schools. Most avoided moving down this line, a position that was possible where this was not essential to the federation's operation. Where a single budget was desirable or necessary, as was the case for 'hard' federations with a statutory basis, schools had to face the issue head on and this hit at the heart of their autonomy.

6.4.2 Reflecting on Leadership

The relationship between head teacher leadership and school effectiveness has been demonstrated in numerous studies over several decades (Teddlie & Reynolds, 2000). Findings from this study indicate that the success of a federation depends on the quality of the head teachers involved. This suggests that the quality of head teachers' leadership is not only important in terms of the effectiveness of individual schools, but also for the development of effective collaborations between schools. Head teachers in this study tended to display characteristics of 'system leaders' (Fullan, 2004) by taking an evolutionary theory perspective where they could see the benefit of collaboration for both individual organisations and the wider system (Alter & Hage, 1993).

The leadership structures put in place varied across the federations. Some appointed a federation director (the titles varied) but these typically had a facilitating role with few delegated powers. This reflected both the nature of the federations and also the lack of clarity about the legal aspects of federation headship that continued throughout the study. For example, the federation that comprised three schools combining on a single campus moved from a structure of three head teacher posts plus federation director to a new structure by the summer of 2006 when the resignation of the last head teacher allowed the federation director to take on the legal status of head teacher. The issue of legal status of the leadership and governance of federations is an important issue and the development of the 2007 School Governance (Federations) (England) Regulations (DfES, 2006) appears to go some way to providing a stronger framework.

It has been argued that one of the original policy drivers for federations was the view that there were insufficient potential head teachers of the necessary quality to lead the country's schools (Glatter & Harvey, 2006). The development of a system where a leader could have responsibility for two or more schools appears to be a response to this view. However, the federations in the present study generally did not set up models that reflected this. As noted, federation leaders tended to have facilitating roles, and in some cases a head teacher of a federation school took on the role because of the failure to appoint. Typically this was seen as *primus inter pares*. As such it reflected a very different model compared to that given above in a 'harder' federation, or that exhibited in one of the federations that withdrew from the study, where there was an executive head with a powerful role over the constituent schools.

Models of distributive leadership within schools have some applicability in federations, but there are further issues to consider. As we have shown, the federations varied in how they were governed and led; the distribution of leadership was not necessarily similar to the way that responsibility is delegated in a school. Rather, the general model was for the schools to continue to have autonomy—federations frequently stressed how important this was to their functioning—under the facilitation of the federation director—although in some federations there was evidence of a greater degree of distributed leadership.

It is increasingly clear that successful interventions and school improvement efforts involve mutual adaptation and are co-constructed (Datnow et al., 2002). The coherence around localised ownership and control combined with the range of models of governance, leadership and management suggests the federations' policy has provided a tight/loose framework which can support the localised development of governance, leadership, and management with the power to serve complex local contexts. In short, the movement towards a federated system may signal the beginnings of a genuine shift towards relocating innovation closer to schools in order to generate greater collective capacity for change. If we can move innovation closer to schools, the opportunity exists to generate locally devised improvement strategies that are relevant to their individualised contexts.

Chapter 7
The Impact of Federations on Student Achievement

7.1 Introduction

In the previous chapter we introduced the concept of a federation, a formal collaborative arrangement between schools that statutorily exists in the English system. In that, and previous, chapters, we have also touched quite a number of times on the perceived advantages of networks and collaboratives in education. However, the bottom line for any educational intervention must be the extent to which it has a positive impact on pupil outcomes. Of course, such outcomes can be varied. Self-esteem, well-being, citizenship, and a disposition towards lifelong learning have all, at various times, been mentioned as goals of schooling and education (Muijs & Reynolds, 2010). However, there exist to our knowledge no education systems where the acquisition of cognitive skills as measured through pupil achievement is not a core goal of the system. The question therefore arises of the extent to which networking and collaboration may positively impact on these outcomes. We have discussed what evidence there is on this in Chapter 1, but as we pointed out in that chapter there is a dearth of evidence on impact on pupil learning and achievement. In this chapter we will explore this question by looking at the relationship between being part of a federation and pupil achievement in English schools, using quantitative methodologies.

7.2 Methods

7.2.1 Researching the Relationship Between Federations and Student Outcomes: Aims and Objectives

The aim of this study is to investigate the ways in which federations seek to improve student outcomes and leadership capacity and the extent of variation in their impact and abilities to promote change. The study also explores factors that facilitating positive impacts of federations and any that act as barriers to improvement and examine whether some models are more effective than others in promoting better outcomes. The specific objectives of this study are to:

D. Muijs et al., *Collaboration and Networking in Education*,
DOI 10.1007/978-94-007-0283-7_7, © Springer Science+Business Media B.V. 2011

1. Investigate changes in student outcomes for federation in terms of key attainment indicators and value added measures and compare these to national trends and results for schools with similar intake characteristics;
2. Assess the impact of federations on leadership capacity and effectiveness; and
3. Assess the impact of federations on the quality of teaching and learning.

7.2.2 Researching the Relationship Between Federations and Student Outcomes: Defining a Research Approach

Our broad approach has been to develop a matched sample of schools in federations and non-federations and conduct quantitative analyses to obtain measures of the apparent impact federations have had on the changes in the educational outcomes of different groups of students over the time (1–4 years). Our approach has involved identifying schools that federated in academic years 2007–2008, 2006–2007, 2005–2006, 2004–2005, and 2003–2004 and comparing the examination performance of cohorts prior to federating with examination performance since federation in terms of key indicators such as %5+ A*–C with and without English and Mathematics, and in value added and contextual value added. In addition, each federation has been matched to a comparator 'non-federation' (in terms of key statistics including those related to pupil intake, rural/urban location, previous attainment profiles) to assess the impact of federating. The following section details the methods used to collect and analyse the data.

7.2.3 Methods

A quantitative methodology was used to explore the relationship between school federations and student performance. National pupil and school level datasets were collected from the Department for Children Schools and Families (DCSF) (now department for Education) to allow us to look at performance measures controlled for student background over time. PLASC and National Pupil Database data were requested from and provided by DCSF for this purpose. Data were collected for each year from 2001 to 2008. Ofsted inspection gradings were provided by the National College for School Leadership. As no definitive central list of federations existed when the study was conducted, a random sample of 50 Local Authorities was selected. Each local authority was contacted by the members of the research team with the request to identify federations and the schools that were a part of them. A total of 264 schools and 122 federations were identified in this way.

Follow up telephone calls were made to each of the schools to ascertain whether there were any errors in the designation of the school as a federation and to collect additional data on date the schools federated, the number of heads, and federation structures. A number of schools/federations were identified that had ceased to operate or did not fit the criteria for federation. These were replaced with other schools/federations.

In order to look at the impact of federation on performance, we opted for a quasi-experimental design where each federation school was matched using propensity score matching to a school as similar as possible on key characteristics prior to federating. National datasets were used to match schools on a number of criteria, including:

1. Phase (e.g. primary, middle, and secondary).
2. Type of school (e.g. Voluntary Aided, Voluntary Controlled, and Academy).
3. Gender intake (co-educational, single sex boys, and single sex girls).
4. Performance levels (e.g. percentage achieving KS threshold levels in English and Maths).
5. Pupil intake characteristics (percentage pupils identified as having Special Educational Needs, percentage pupils eligible for Free School Meals).
6. Location (this measure went beyond traditional rural/urban identification, and attempted to match areas that were as similar as possible on socio-demographic characteristics. For example, Cambridge would be matched to York and Salford to Gateshead).
7. School size (as indicated by pupil roll).

Clearly, no schools could be matched identically on these criteria. However, as close a match as possible was sought in all cases. As with the federation schools, all comparator schools were contacted by a member of the research team to ascertain that they were not themselves in a federation and to collect data on Headship and governance. As a result of this, a number of schools had to be replaced as they were themselves part of a federation or had ceased to operate. A range of quantitative methodologies were used to analyse the data (see results section), including univariate and multivariate statistics and multilevel modelling. The Stata and MLWin software packages were used for these analyses.

7.2.4 Sampling

The final sample contained a total of 50 LAs, and 264 schools. These are grouped into 122 federations. Two hundred sixty-four comparator schools were selected to match these. A total of 88.1% of schools in the sample belonged to a two-school federation, 8.5% were part of a three-school federation, with the remainder being part of larger federations. The distribution of schools across phases was (Table 7.1):

A total of 11.3% of schools were Catholic, 16.2% were CofE, and 4.1% were Academies.

The federations tended to have been formed relatively recently, reflecting a rapid development in this area (Table 7.2):

Most federations in the sample were formed in either 2007 or 2008, with just over a quarter formed in 2005 or earlier. Of total federations surveyed, 80.97% had

Table 7.1 Distribution of schools across phases in percentages

Nursery	3.8
Infant	7.2
Junior	7.2
Primary	39.6
First	9.0
Middle	5.3
High	1.9
Secondary	22.3
Special	3.7

Table 7.2 Formation year

Year formed	Percentage
2001 and earlier	1.79
2002	0.00
2003	0.00
2004	1.79
2005	4.46
2006	17.86
2007	32.59
2008	33.48
2009	8.04

a joint head teacher, 19.03% had not. Of total federations surveyed, 14.6% had a joint governing body, 85.6% had not (Table 7.3).

Almost half of the schools surveyed had had only one Head in the past 5 years, with over a third having had two. There were very few differences between federation and comparator schools in this regard.

Table 7.3 Number of head teachers in the past 5 years

Number of heads in last 5 years	% Federation schools	% Comparator schools
1	49.55	49.54
2	35.59	38.99
3	10.36	9.17
4	3.6	1.94
5	0.9	0.46

7.2.5 Federation and Comparator School Characteristics

Federation and comparator schools were compared on key intake variables. Schools were exactly matched on:

- School type
- Gender intake
- Phase

Table 7.4 Characteristics of federation and comparator schools on key variables

	Federation mean	Comparator mean	*t*
School roll	287.9	281.4	−0.74
Percentage pupils with SEN	30.2	31.6	1.35
Percentage reaching threshold targets in English	79.2	77.9	0.98
Percentage reaching threshold targets in Maths	74.3	76.8	1.96*

* Significant difference at the 0.05 level.

Table 7.4 depicts match for the variables school roll, SEN percentage, FSM percentage.

The only significant difference found was on Maths achievement, where comparator schools significantly outperformed federation schools, though the difference was small.

7.3 Results

7.3.1 A Typology of Federations

The data was interrogated to find types of federations. Six different types of federations were identified:

a. *Cross-Phase Federations* – Federations consisting of two or more schools of different phases, e.g. a primary and secondary school, or a First, Middle, and High school. Of total schools in the sample, 35.1% are part of this type of federation.
b. *Performance Federations* – Federations consisting of 2 or more schools, some of which are low performing, and others high performing, usually two schools. Of total schools, 15.6% are part of this type of federation.
c. *Size Federations* – Federations consisting of two or more very small or small schools, or a small school and a medium-sized school. Of total schools, 18.8% are part of this type of federation.
d. *Mainstreaming Federations* – One or more special schools combine with one or more mainstream schools. Of total schools in the sample, 4.6% are part of this type of federation.
e. *Faith Federations* – Two or more schools of the same denomination combine. This type can overlap with one of the other four types, but in many cases does not. Of total schools in the sample, 14.8% are part of this type of federation
f. *Academy Federations* – Two or more Academies run by the same sponsor form a federation. Of total schools, 2.3% are a part of this type of federation.

A total of 7.8% of schools were in federations that were not immediately classifiable.

7.3.2 Federations and Impact on Performance

Multilevel statistical models were used to look at the impact of federation on performance. This was done only for the cohorts of federations formed in 2005 and earlier and 2006, as no impact is to be expected for those federations formed in 2007 and later in light of previous research on the length of time it takes for federations to become fully operational (see Lindsay et al., 2005). Levels were school (level 2) and pupil (level 1). As the data relates to different cohorts in different years analysis of each year was done separately.

Models were tested for the year of formation and 3 years prior data combined, and for subsequent years up to 2008. A null model was formulated with no predictors. In the next model federation was added, while in the final model for each year other correlates of achievement were included, such as gender, SEN status, and FSM eligibility. Outcome variables were pupil-level achievement, such a KS levels or % 5A*–C grades. As our variable of interest was a school-level variables, all predictors in the analyses are school-level variables.

7.4 2005 Cohort

In the 2005 cohort analyses are only presented for the primary phase (KS2), due to the fact that the sample of secondary schools for this cohort was at four (making a total of eight schools including comparators) too small to provide stable estimates.

Tables 7.5, 7.6, and 7.7 show that for the 2005 cohort there is some evidence of impact of federations over time. Overall, the majority of the variance in both English

Table 7.5 Baseline multilevel models 2005 cohort

	English – null model – coefficient (standard error)	English – full model – coefficient (standard error)	Maths – null model – coefficient (standard error)	Maths – full model – coefficient (standard error)
Intercept	9.46 (3.86)	12.3 (5.38)	6.1 (2.7)	5.89 (3.8)
Federated?		NS		NS
Gender		NS		NS
Age		NS		NS
FSM		NS		NS
SEN		NS		NS
School size		NS		NS
Level 2 percentage variance	11.7	11.2	12.3	12.1
Level 1 percentage variance	88.3	88.8	87.7	87.9
Explained percentage variance level 2		5.3%		3.2%
Explained percentage variance level 1		0.0%		0.0%
Total percentage explained variance		0.6%		0.2%

NS = Variable not significant.

Table 7.6 2006 Multilevel models 2005 cohort

	English – null model – coefficient (standard error)	English – full model – coefficient (standard error)	Maths – null model – coefficient (standard error)	Maths – full model – coefficient (standard error)
Intercept	5.1 (1.3)	12.3 (5.38)	5.1 (0.4)	10.2 (3.8)
Federated?		NS		2.5 (1.1)
Gender		NS		NS
Age		NS		NS
FSM		NS		NS
SEN		NS		NS
School size		NS		NS
Level 2 percentage variance	10.8	10.2	12.8	9.5
Level 1 percentage variance	89.2	89.8	87.2	92.5
Explained percentage variance level 2		4.7%		36.5%
Explained percentage variance level 1		0.0%		1.2%
Total percentage explained variance		0.4%		4.7%

NS = Variable not significant.

Table 7.7 2007 Multilevel models 2005 cohort

	English – null model – coefficient (standard error)	English – full model – coefficient (standard error)	Maths – null model – coefficient (standard error)	Maths – full model – coefficient (standard error)
Intercept	6.4 (1.1)	5.6 (1.0)	5.1 (0.4)	10.2 (3.8)
Federated?		3.1 (1.4)		3.8 (1.1)
Gender		NS		NS
Age		NS		NS
FSM		NS		NS
SEN		NS		NS
School size		NS		NS
Level 2 percentage variance	14.9	9.4%	12.8	7.5
Level 1 percentage variance	85.1	90.6	87.2	92.5
Explained percentage variance level 2		38.9%		46.5%
Explained percentage variance level 1		0.0%		1.2%
Total percentage explained variance		6.1%		6.6%

NS = Variable not significant.

Table 7.8 Baseline multilevel measures 2006 cohort primary

	English – null model – coefficient (standard error)	English – full model – coefficient (standard error)	Maths – null model – coefficient (standard error)	Maths – full model – coefficient (standard error)
Intercept	4.2 (0.03)	4.6 (0.09)	4.1 (0.4)	4.3 (0.1)
Federated?		NS		NS
Gender		NS		NS
Age		NS		NS
FSM		NS		NS
SEN		–0.015 (0.005)		–0.009 (0.004)
School size		NS		NS
Level 2 percentage variance	12.8	10.2	15.4	13.9
Level 1 percentage variance	87.2	89.8	84.6	86.1
Explained percentage variance level 2		4.7%		5.2%
Explained percentage variance level 1		0.0%		0.2%
Total percentage explained variance		0.4%		0.7%

NS = Variable not significant.

and Maths is explained at the pupil level (level 1). However, variance at the school level is also significant. It is important here to point out that pupil level variance is not the same thing as pupil social background, as is often wrongly supposed. Rather, this may be a range of factors, including ability, motivation, and, to a large extent, measurement error.

As the samples were carefully matched on these variables, it is not surprising that most predictors were not significantly related to the outcomes. Federation is significantly related to outcomes in Maths in 2006 and 2007, and to outcomes in English in 2007. This is suggestive of impact, although other factors, such as prior capacity to change in federation as opposed to non-federation schools may of course be a causal factor as well. The impact of federation is quite strong in 2007, explaining nearly half of school level variance in Maths, and over a third of school level variance in English, making it a highly significant factor.

7.5 2006 Cohort

(i) Primary (Tables 7.8, 7.9, 7.10, and 7.11)

For cohort 2006 we can again see some evidence of impact of federations over time. Overall, the majority of the variance in both English and Maths is explained at the pupil level (level 1). However, variance at the school level is also significant and slightly larger for this cohort than for the 2005 cohort.

Table 7.9 2007 Multilevel models 2006 cohort primary

	English – null model – coefficient (standard error)	English – full model – coefficient (standard error)	Maths – null model – coefficient (standard error)	Maths – full model – coefficient (standard error)
Intercept	7.6 (1.3)	8.7 (0.7)	5.3 (0.6)	6.5 (0.8)
Federated?		2.4 (0.9)		3.1 (1.1)
Gender		NS		NS
Age		NS		NS
FSM		NS		NS
SEN		0.02 (0.01)		0.016 (0.007)
Number of heads		NS		NS
Level 2 percentage variance	13.2%	11.1%	15.8	12.7
Level 1 percentage variance	86.8	88.9	84.2	87.3
Explained percentage variance level 2		19.9%		22.7%
Explained percentage variance level 1		0.0%		0.%
Total percentage explained variance		2.3%		2.8%

NS = Variable not significant.

The variables on which the samples were matched were in general not significantly related to the outcomes. However, there was a weak significant relationship between percentage pupils with SEN and outcomes. Federation is significantly related to outcomes in English and Maths in 2007, and not at baseline. This is suggestive of impact, as again there appears to be an increase in impact over time. The impact of federation is quite strong in 2007, explaining nearly around 20% of the variance in outcomes.

Table 7.10 Baseline multilevel models 2006 cohort secondary

	Average points score at GCSE – null model	Average points score at GCSE – full model
Intercept	10.42 (0.22)	12.0 (0.94)
Federated?		NS
Gender		NS
Age		NS
FSM		NS
SEN		NS
School size		NS
Level 2 percentage variance	17.6%	16.2
Level 1 percentage variance	82.4	83.8
Explained percentage variance level 2		3.8%
Explained percentage variance level 1		0.2%
Total percentage explained variance		0.7%

NS = Variable not significant.

Table 7.11 2007 Multilevel models 2006 cohort secondary

	Average points score at GCSE – null model	Average points score at GCSE – full model
Intercept	7.6 (1.3)	8.0 (0.6)
Federated?		5.4 (2.6)
Gender		NS
Age		NS
FSM		NS
SEN		NS
Number of heads		NS
Level 2 percentage variance	19.0%	15.7%
Level 1 percentage variance	81.0	84.3
Explained percentage variance level 2		20.5%
Explained percentage variance level 1		0.0%
Total percentage explained variance		3.9%

NS = Variable not significant.

(ii) Secondary

Similar results are found for GCSE. Overall, the majority of the variance in both English and Maths is explained at the pupil level (level 1), with between 15 and 20% of the variance being at the school level.

As in the primary schools, most predictors were not significantly related to the outcomes. Federation is significantly related to outcomes in 2007, and not in 2006. This is suggestive of impact, as again there appears to be an increase in impact over time. The impact of federation is quite strong in 2007, explaining around 20% of the variance in outcomes.

7.5.1 Impact on Performance by Federation Type

In this section we will look at performance in the different types of federations. As sample sizes at level 2 (school level) are small in many cases, multilevel estimates may be unstable. Therefore we have used simple bivariate analyses to explore this question, which we would be able to interrogate in more detail if we had a larger sample of schools.

7.6 2005 Cohort

a. Cross-Phase Federation (Tables 7.12 and 7.13)

While no differences were found between federations and comparator schools at baseline, in 2006 and 2007 federation schools showed higher levels of performance than comparator schools.

Table 7.12 Cross-Phase federations – English

	Federation mean	Comparator mean	t
Baseline	4.1	3.8	−3.6
2006	4.2	3.6	−6.5**
2007	4.2	3.7	−5.7**

* = Significant at the 0.05 level, ** = significant at the 0.01 level, *** = significant at the 0.001 level.

Table 7.13 Cross-Phase federations – Maths

	Federation mean	Comparator mean	t
Baseline	4.0	3.7	−4.0
2006	4.2	3.6	−5.7**
2007	4.3	3.6	−5.9**

* = Significant at the 0.05 level, ** = significant at the 0.01 level, *** = significant at the 0.001 level.

Table 7.14 Size federations – English

	Federation mean	Comparator mean	t
Baseline	4.3	4.2	−1.0
2006	4.3	4.1	−1.2
2007	4.4	4.0	−2.1

* = Significant at the 0.05 level, ** = significant at the 0.01 level, *** = significant at the 0.001 level.

Table 7.15 Size federations – Maths

	Federation mean	Comparator mean	t
Baseline	4.2	4.2	0.0
2006	4.3	4.2	−0.7
2007	4.3	4.1	−1.1

* = Significant at the 0.05 level, ** = significant at the 0.01 level, *** = significant at the 0.001 level.

b. Size Federations (Tables 7.14 and 7.15)

No significant differences were found for size federations.

Performance, Mainstreaming, and Faith federations were too few in number in this cohort for us to conduct analyses.

The tables above show that there is evidence that Cross-Phase federations may have a positive impact on performance, in that a federation schools in this category outperform comparison schools in years 2006 and 2007, but not 2005, but there is no evidence for size federations. The sample size for size federations was smaller, however.

7.7 2006 Cohort

(i) Primary

a. Cross-Phase Federation (Tables 7.16 and 7.17)

Table 7.16 Cross-Phase federations – English

	Federation mean	Comparator mean	*t*
Baseline	4.1	4.1	0.0
2007	4.1	4.0	2.7

* = Significant at the 0.05 level, ** = significant at the 0.01 level, *** = significant at the 0.001 level.

Table 7.17 Cross-Phase federations – Maths

	Federation mean	Comparator mean	*t*
Baseline	4.0	4.0	0.1
2007	4.0	4.0	0.3

* = Significant at the 0.05 level, ** = significant at the 0.01 level, *** = significant at the 0.001 level.

No significant differences were found for Cross-Phase federations in primary for the 2006 cohort.

b. Performance Federations (Tables 7.18 and 7.19)

Table 7.18 Performance federations – English

	Federation mean	Comparator mean	*t*
Baseline	4.1	4.1	0.1
2007	4.2	3.8	2.9**

* = Significant at the 0.05 level, ** = significant at the 0.01 level, *** = significant at the 0.001 level.

While no differences were found at baseline, in 2007 attainment in performance federations was significantly higher than in comparator schools in 2007.

Table 7.19 Performance federations – Maths

	Federation mean	Comparator mean	*T*
Baseline	4.1	4.2	1.0
2007	4.3	3.7	4.1***

* = Significant at the 0.05 level, ** = significant at the 0.01 level, *** = significant at the 0.001 level.

c. Size Federations (Tables 7.20 and 7.21)

Table 7.20 Size federations – English

	Federation mean	Comparator mean	*t*
Baseline	4.1	4.4	–2.5*
2007	4.0	4.2	–1.5

* = Significant at the 0.05 level, ** = significant at the 0.01 level, *** = significant at the 0.001 level.

Table 7.21 Size federations – Maths

	Federation mean	Comparator mean	*t*
Baseline	4.1	4.3	–1.2
2007	4.0	4.1	–0.8

* = Significant at the 0.05 level, ** = significant at the 0.01 level, *** = significant at the 0.001 level.

Comparator schools showed higher performance than federation schools in English at baseline. No other significant differences were found.

d. Faith Federations (Tables 7.22 and 7.23)

Table 7.22 Faith federations – English

	Federation mean	Comparator mean	*t*
Baseline	4.1	4.1	−0.2
2007	4.1	3.9	1.2

* = Significant at the 0.05 level, ** = significant at the 0.01 level, *** = significant at the 0.001 level.

Table 7.23 Faith federations – Maths

	Federation mean	Comparator mean	t
Baseline	4.1	4.0	0.7
2007	4.0	3.9	0.5

* = Significant at the 0.05 level, ** = significant at the 0.01 level, *** = significant at the 0.001 level.

No significant differences were found for Faith federations.

Mainstreaming federations were too few in number in this cohort for us to conduct analyses.

The only significant differences found were for Performance federations in 2007 in both English and Maths, where students outperformed their counterparts in the comparison schools (this had not been the case at baseline), and for Size federations in English at baseline, where comparator schools did better than federation schools. This was no longer the case in 2007.

Overall, it would appear that the main differences in performance between federation and comparator schools appear in Performance federations. The evidence for Cross-Phase federations is mixed, while few or no significant differences were found for the other types. It has to be pointed out though that in many cases sample sizes were too small to include particular federation types in the analyses.

(ii) Secondary

a. Cross-Phase Federation (Table 7.24)

Table 7.24 Cross-Phase federations

	Federation mean	Comparator mean	t
Baseline	341.5	351.8	–3.8***
2007	341.2	353.9	–2.6**

* = Significant at the 0.05 level, ** = significant at the 0.01 level, *** = significant at the 0.001 level.

b. Performance Federation (Table 7.25)

Table 7.25 Performance federations

	Federation mean	Comparator mean	t
Baseline	295.6	274.8	1.9
2007	324.9	251.4	12.3***

* = Significant at the 0.05 level, ** = significant at the 0.01 level, *** = significant at the 0.001 level.

Notably in the secondary sample only Cross-Phase and Performance federations were present in sufficient numbers for analysis. In Cross-Phase federations, Comparator schools showed significantly higher levels of performance in both years. For Performance federations, there was a non-significant advantage for Performance schools at baseline, and a highly significant advantage for Performance schools in 2007.

Overall, it would appear that the main differences in performance between federation and comparator schools appear in Performance federations. The evidence for Cross-Phase federations is mixed, while few or no significant differences were found for the other types. It has to be pointed out though that in many cases sample sizes were too small to include particular federation types in the analyses.

7.7.1 Relationship with Ofsted Grades

In this section we will explore the extent to which there is a relationship between federation and Ofsted inspection grades. In view of sample size issues all types and phases of schools have been combined. It has to be pointed out here that as inspection does not occur on an annual basis in each school comparisons refer to different schools in different years, so any findings have to be considered indicative only (Tables 7.26, 7.27, and 7.28).

Table 7.26 2005 Inspections

Variable	Federated	Comparison	*t*
Overall effectiveness of provision	4.8	4.6	−0.6
Quality of teaching	3.6	3.5	−0.2
How well do learners achieve?	3.3	3.2	−0.1
Overall effectiveness of leadership and management	3.0	3.3	1.0

Table 7.27 2006 Inspections

Variable	Federated	Comparison	*t*
Overall effectiveness of provision	3.5	3.6	−0.1
Quality of teaching	2.4	2.4	0.1
How well do learners achieve?	2.5	2.5	0.2
Overall effectiveness of leadership and management	2.3	2.4	0.7

Table 7.28 2007 Inspections

Variable	Federated	Comparison	t
Overall effectiveness of provision	2.5	2.5	0.2
Quality of teaching	2.6	2.5	0.4
How well do learners achieve?	2.3	2.4	0.6
Overall effectiveness of leadership and management	2.1	2.1	−0.1

No significant differences were found between federation and comparison schools in any of the comparisons made for inspection ratings. However, it has to be pointed out that sample sizes were small.

7.7.2 Summary of Results

In conclusion we summarise the five key findings.

1. This study has identified six broad and sometimes overlapping categories of federation:

    - Size Federations
    - Cross-Phase Federations
    - Performance Federations
    - Faith Federations
    - Mainstreaming Federations
    - Academy groups

    The most popular category of federation in the sample is Cross-Phase federation and the least popular category is Academy groups.
2. There is evidence of impact on overall performance, in that while federation and comparator schools perform similarly at baseline, Federation is positively related to performance in the years following federation.
3. There is evidence to suggest that impact is strongest in Performance federations.
4. There is no relationship between federation and Ofsted judgements (grades).
5. There is no evidence of differential impact on students from different socio-economic settings, differences in gender, or with special educational needs.

7.8 Conclusion

Our analysis leads us to conclude that federations can have a positive impact on student outcomes and the federation impact is strongest where the aim of the federation is to raise educational standards by federating higher and lower attaining schools. This initial analysis would suggest persisting with the policy of federating schools to raise standards is a worthwhile enterprise.

However, if federations are to continue to be used as a structural solution we would draw attention to three major challenges within the system:

1. The challenge of stimulating and developing collaboration both within and between schools in very challenging contexts.
2. The challenge of developing appropriate accountability systems that move beyond single institutions as the primary unit of analysis.
3. The challenge of inspiring localised context specific approaches to improvement within an overarching national framework of intervention, such as the National Challenge.

We suggest these challenges need further exploration, including discussions with performance federation leaders to draw out the key issues related to the three challenges and the facilitators and barriers experienced while establishing a federation.

Chapter 8
Achieving Excellence and Equity: Reflections on the Development of Practices in One Local District Over 10 Years

As education systems in many countries respond to demands for higher standards, they face the challenge of how to achieve equity. Put simply, how can systems continue to raise overall levels of achievement whilst reducing the gap between higher- and lower-performing groups of learners?

This chapter reflects on evidence collected as a result of a series of studies, all carried out in one English local education authority, to address this agenda. This programme of research was unusual in that it tracked developments over 10 years. The findings point to the potential of processes of networking between schools as a possible way forward. At the same time, they also reveal how the implementation of such collaborative approaches presents difficulties, particularly within a policy context that emphasises competition between schools as the main driver for reform.

The chapter concludes that progress in mobilising the potential of networking requires new thinking within schools, not least in terms of leadership practice and the use of evidence as a stimulus for experimentation; new relationships between schools and their district level administrations; and national policies that will encourage such changes to occur.

Before examining what happened in the particular local authority over the 10-year period, I begin by outlining the policy context, and the overall theoretical and methodological perspectives that were used in carrying out the programme of research.

8.1 The Policy Context

Since the Labour government came to office in 1997, the main focus of education in England has been on what has come to be called 'the standards agenda', an approach to educational reform which seeks to 'drive up' standards of attainment, including workforce skill levels and ultimately national competitiveness in a globalised economy (Lipman, 2004). The vigour with which this agenda has been pursued has led some American commentators to describe England as a 'laboratory' for educational reform (Finkelstein & Grubb, 2000).

The government has argued that the raising of standards *is* about equity: that a powerful emphasis on raising attainment will not simply benefit children who

D. Muijs et al., *Collaboration and Networking in Education*,
DOI 10.1007/978-94-007-0283-7_8,

are already performing at a high level but is of even greater benefit to previously low-attaining children in poorly performing schools (Blunkett, 1999). In practice, however, the standards agenda has concentrated on a narrow view of attainment in a way that has tended to discourage the participation and learning of some groups of learners. It has also been linked to other aspects of policy that can have perverse effects, such as the marketisation of education; a directive relationship between government and schools that potentially bypasses the participation of teachers in their own work and disengages schools from their local communities; and a regime of target setting and inspection, creating an 'accountability culture' to force up standards (O'Neill, 2002). Meanwhile, schools have been expected to play their part in tackling 'social exclusion' (Blair, 1997; Social Exclusion Unit, 2001) by ensuring that everyone—and not just the highest attainers, or those from the most advantaged backgrounds—is equipped to compete in an ever-more-demanding labour market.

It is not surprising, therefore, that the English education system has been the scene of significant tensions. Since schools are held to account for the attainments of their students and are required to make themselves attractive to families who are most able to exercise choice of school for their children, low-attaining students, students who demand high levels of attention and resource, and those who are seen not to conform to school and classroom behavioural norms, are unattractive to many schools. Giroux and Schmidt (2004) explain how similar reforms in the United States have turned some schools into 'test-prep centres'. As a result, they tend to be increasingly ruthless in their disregard of those students who pose a threat to success, as determined by measured forms of assessment.

Nevertheless, policies for excellence and equity are not seen as standing in contradiction to one another, but as constituting 'two sides of the same coin' (Brehony & Deem, 2003). Rather than making fundamental choices between these two agendas, therefore, the concern of policy makers is to find specific strategies which will enable both to be pursued simultaneously.

8.2 Making Sense of Practice

This complex English policy context has provided researchers with opportunities to study what has possibly been the most intensive attempt so far to bring about system-wide improvements in relation to notions of excellence and equity. Much of the recent work of my colleagues and I has been focussed on this agenda (see Ainscow & West, 2006). It has mainly involved the use of *Development and Research* (D&R), an approach that we have been developing in recent years. It involves practitioners working in partnership with academics in order to develop better understandings of educational processes (Ainscow, Dyson, Goldrick, & Kerr, 2009). Lewin's dictum that you cannot understand an organisation until you try to change it is, perhaps, the clearest justification for this approach (Schein, 2001).

In practical terms, we believe that such understandings are best developed as a result of 'outsiders', such as ourselves, in working alongside teachers, head teachers, local authority staff, and other stakeholders as they attempt to move practice forward by seeking practical solutions to the complex problems posed by policy implementation. We argue that this approach can be used to overcome the traditional gap between research and practice.

As we have refined our understanding of the idea of D&R, we have come to see it as a process of knowledge-generation, occurring when researcher and practitioner perspectives come together in particular sites. The overall aim is to produce new knowledge about ways in which broad values, such as equity, might better be realised in future practice. Whilst this conceptualisation draws on notions of *action research*—particularly, critical collaborative action research—and of *research and development*, it does not equate precisely with either. Unlike action research, it is not focussed simply on particular sites, but seeks to generate transferable knowledge. Unlike research and development, it does not assume that the contribution of researchers to this process is prior to that of practitioners. In other words, researchers do not design practices that are then implemented by practitioners.

This leads us to see researchers not as pre-hoc designers but as ad-hoc supporters and post-hoc model builders. Our role is to support practitioners in developing the best possible propositions about what will promote improvements in a given situation. This involves bringing to bear knowledge gained from prior research, but, given the uniqueness of particular situations and the general nature of values, this cannot amount to a 'design'. Moreover, what emerges from practitioners' attempts to act on these propositions is not a finely tuned and context-independent set of practices which can be transferred wholesale to other sites. Rather, the practices developed in one site, together with their underpinning rationale, become an elaborated set of propositions to be put forward in other sites. We call these elaborated propositions 'models', and the whole process we refer to as one of development and research in order to emphasise the different relationship between the two terms from that implied by 'research and development'.

In what follows, I summarise and reflect on a series of three linked studies that involved a D&R approach, all carried out in partnership with colleagues in 'Tramton', one of the most deprived local authorities in England. This programme of activities took place during a period when this local authority came to be recognised nationally for its success in promoting school improvement. In 1997, Tramton was described by Ofsted, the national inspection agency, as having 'a formidable legacy of under-performance'. Subsequently, it has made great strides in developing the performance of its schools in relation to its motto, 'Aiming High, Including All'.

As my colleagues and I worked alongside practitioners, trying to make sense of what happened in Tramton, we found ourselves using the idea of *communities of practice* as a theoretical framework for examining the ways in which those involved attempted to collaborate in addressing common areas of concern. The idea of communities of practice emerged out of traditions of sociocultural and situative theories of learning (Lave & Wenger, 1991). Like others, we have found it a helpful means of examining what happens when groups of people work together on educational change efforts (e.g. Mitra, 2008). A limitation of its use, however, is its lack of attention to the role of power in such contexts (Brown & Duguid, 2000), a factor that emerges as I re-trace developments in Tramton.

Our involvement in Tramton can be seen in relation to three overlapping phases of development, as follows:

- Phase 1 (1997–2001)—Raising Standards
- Phase 2 (2001–2004)—Fostering Inclusion
- Phase 3 (2004–2007)—Networking Across the Authority

I will consider each of these phases in turn, summarising and reflecting on the evidence we collected. Further details about each of the studies are already available in earlier publications.

8.3 Phase 1 (1997–2001)—Raising Standards

Local Education Authorities (LEAs) in England are accountable to their electorates and to the Secretary of State for maintained schools in their areas. However, in recent years national reforms have gradually eroded the power of LEAs. The stated aim has been to delegate greater responsibility to the level of schools in the belief that this will help to foster improvements in standards.

As we worked along LEA staff in Tramton between 1997 and 2001, shadowing, observing, and interviewing those involved, we saw how they responded to this changing policy context by developing new relationships with schools.[1] During that period there was increasing evidence that the authority's strategy was paying off (Ainscow & Howes, 2001). Test and examination results rose across all phases of the service, with improvement rates in primary sector tests amongst the highest nationally. And, whilst over the period the LEA had up to 15 schools either requiring special measures or having serious weaknesses as a result of inspections carried out by Ofsted (the national inspection agency), by early 2001 the figures were down to just two with serious weaknesses. In addition, some schools that had previously been in crisis subsequently received positive inspection reports. As a result, in its inspection report on the LEA, Ofsted stated, 'This is a remarkable, unique record that is not paralleled elsewhere in the country'.

School Improvement Officers. Our research focussed specifically on the work of the team of school consultants, known as School Improvement Officers (SIOs), that was the authority's support arm (Ainscow, Howes, & Tweddle, 2006). The evidence we collected through shadowing their visits to schools and interviewing other stakeholders, left us in no doubt that they were remarkably creative in inventing ways of working that stimulated and supported change within schools. However, we remained unconvinced that simply lifting these approaches in order to reproduce them in a different context would have the powerful impact that they clearly had within the particular LEA. The problem with such an approach is that it overlooks

[1] I monitored the first phase of development with my colleague Andy Howes as an evaluation commissioned by the local authority. It involved the shadowing of staff, observations of meetings, and a programme of individual interviews with stakeholders (see Ainscow & Howes, 2001).

the social processes of learning that enabled the strategies to have their powerful impact. Consequently, we reflected further on our evidence in order to seek a deeper understanding of what was involved in these 'social processes of learning'.

Wenger (1998) provides a framework that can be used to analyse learning in social contexts. At the centre of this framework is the concept of a *community of practice*, a social group engaged in the sustained pursuit of a shared enterprise. This suggests that practices are ways of negotiating meaning through social action. Wenger argues that learning within a given community can often be best explained within the intertwining of reification and participation. He suggests that these are complementary processes, in that each has the capacity to repair the ambiguity of meaning the other can engender. So, for example, we observed how particular strategies would be developed as part of SIO planning activities and summarised in a set of guidance for action, providing a codified reification of intended practice. However, the meaning and practical implications of these strategies only became clear as they were tried in the field and discussed between colleagues. In this way, participation resulted in social learning that could not be produced solely by reification alone. At the same time, the reified products, such as the policy documents that emerged, served as a kind of memory of practice, cementing in place the new learning.

We can, then, use the notion of communities of practice to offer an explanation of what happened in Tramton. It does seem that the key to the LEA's success lay in its success in encouraging networking at different levels within the service. In particular, the links encouraged between head teachers seemed to encourage the creation of many different communities of practice that helped to break down the sense of intellectual and, indeed, emotional isolation that had characterised their previous working lives. Then, through a complex set of strategies and processes, the LEA facilitated participation and reification procedures that helped such learning communities to grow. Such an analysis seems to provide a way of describing the processes that were at the heart of the authority's success. So, to what extent was this consistent with what the Government had in mind for the future of LEAs?

New Roles. An analysis of the new ways in which the Government intended LEAs to operate was presented in the form of a Code of Practice (DfEE, 2001). In particular, LEAs were expected to monitor the performance of their schools, in order to support and challenge them. The Code suggested that monitoring of schools should be based on routinely available information, particularly test data, Ofsted inspection reports and information from school-self review. Indeed, it concluded that an authority which makes effective use of the full range of information which is routinely available to it will rarely need to visit schools solely for the purpose of gathering further information.

Certainly, the SIOs in our study saw themselves as supporting and, where necessary, challenging school-led improvement strategies. However, all of this was set within a wider context of relationships and procedures that meant that they had developed a deep knowledge of what went on in the schools. In this way they were able to engage senior school staff in detailed discussion of improvement strategies, bringing to bear their detailed knowledge of particular people (staff and pupils), contexts, policies, and practices.

The government's Code of Practice placed enormous emphasis on the LEA's duty to identify and support schools causing concern. It stressed that the prime focus should be to ensure that an effective head teacher and senior management team are in place, working with an effective governing body in pursuit of a good and deliverable action plan. Our observations indicated that it was through their increasingly close knowledge of the schools that SIOs were able to pick up signs that things were not altogether well. In some instances, schools were then placed on the LEA's list of schools causing concern. As a result, it was possible to mobilise additional human resources in order to enable a school to address a growing difficulty.

It is difficult to see how such interventions could be achieved simply through the use of 'routinely available information' of the sort outlined within the Code of Practice. SIOs felt that they knew their schools, and that it was this knowledge which made their interventions authentic. Our interview data indicated that, by and large, head teachers were in agreement.

The Challenge of Including All. Phillips and Harper-Jones (2003) claim that Labour's education policy has been characterised by four themes: 'a determination to raise educational standards; a quest to undertake the modernisation of educational systems, structures, and practices; a commitment to choice and diversity within education; and a preoccupation with the culture of performativity'. However, what possibly differentiated this Labour government from its predecessor was a 'fifth theme', which Phillips and Harper-Jones rather gloss over. That is, a broad commitment to equity in and through education, variously badged as 'inclusion' or 'social inclusion'.

This was arguably the most troubling aspect of what happened in Tramton during the period up to 2001. It revealed how, within a context that valued aggregated test and examination scores and the outcomes of inspection as the sole criteria for determining success, such moves act as a barrier to the development of a more equitable education system.

Towards the end of our study, we interviewed an external consultant who had assisted the LEA in its preparations for its Ofsted inspection, looking specifically at its approach to vulnerable groups of learners. He suggested that salaries within the LEA were evidence of what he saw as 'a pecking order' of officers, influencing the way priorities were signalled within the service. SIOs, he said, were the best-paid people in the department. He went on to describe the difficulties faced by lower status staff, such as educational psychologists or advisory teachers, going into a school to help make some inclusive arrangement for an individual child experiencing difficulties and seen to be pulling in the opposite direction to the SIO.

The consultant told of how, with an Ofsted inspection looming, some SIOs had encouraged various types of informal pupil exclusion, so that classes would become easier to manage. The SIO brief, as he understood it, was to get schools out of special measures very quickly, or to prevent them from going into special measures in the first place. We found evidence of similar experiences, all of which led us to conclude that the apparently successful efforts of this particular LEA to respond to the government's demands for improved standards had, in practice, created barriers to the participation of certain groups of pupils. In other words, people in the authority were 'aiming high' by 'excluding some'. This led us to argue that, within the Tramton school system, there was expertise available that could be used to strengthen equity across the service. However, we also concluded that external pressures were creating barriers that prevented the moving around of this expertise.

During 2000 we were able to stimulate discussion amongst LEA staff as to how they might place more emphasis on making the LEA's school improvement strategy more equitable. In so doing, we argued that the LEA would need a powerful strategy for change in order for it to be successful in addressing this complex set of issues. Such a strategy, we suggested, required the development of effective strategies for making better use of available expertise. All of this helped to create the opportunity for the next phase of our involvement in Tramton.

8.4 Phase 2 (2001–2004)—Fostering Inclusion

The second phase of development focussed on the local authority's continuing desire to 'aim high' and 'include all'. It involved a network of nine schools (primary and secondary) that set out to develop more inclusive ways of working and was part of a larger study funded by the Economic and Social Research Council's Teaching and Learning Research Programme.[2] (see Ainscow, Booth, & Dyson, 2006; Ainscow, Howes, Farrell, & Frankham, 2003; Ainscow, Booth, & Dyson, Farrell, et al., 2006).

Participating schools were invited to explore ways of developing inclusion in their own contexts. SIOs supported the schools as they undertook research to identify the barriers to learning and participation experienced by their students and to find ways to reduce those barriers. The research process varied from site to site in response to local priorities and possibilities. Evidence was gathered by the schools and by university researchers, using observations and interviews.

Becoming Inclusive. What we noted as the developments occurred was neither the crushing of the schools' efforts to become more inclusive by the government's policies for raising standards, nor the rejection of the standards agenda in favour of a radical, inclusive alternative (Ainscow et al., 2006). In most of the schools, the two agendas remained intertwined. Indeed, the focus on attainment appeared to prompt some teachers to examine issues in relation to the achievements and participation of hitherto marginalised groups that they had previously overlooked. Likewise, the concern with inclusion tended to shape the way the school responded to the imperative to raise standards.

In trying to make sense of the relationship between external imperatives and the processes of change in these schools, we once again drew on Wenger's ideas to reveal how external agendas were mediated by the norms and values of the

---

[2]Phase 2 was carried out in partnership with my colleagues Peter Farrell, Andy Howes, and Jo Frankham as part of a larger study funded by the Teaching and Learning Research Programme of the Economic and Social Research Council (Award L139 25 1001).

communities of practice within the schools, and how they become part of a dialogue whose outcomes can be more rather than less inclusive. In this way, the role of national policy emerged from the study in something of a new light. This suggests that schools may be able to engage with what might appear to be unfavourable policy imperatives to produce outcomes that are by no means inevitably non-inclusive.

Our close monitoring of what happened revealed how social learning processes within schools influenced people's action and, indeed, the thinking that informed their actions (Ainscow Howes, Farrell, & Frankham, 2003). Often this was stimulated by various forms of evidence that created a sense of interruption to existing ways of thinking and working. Particularly powerful techniques in this respect involved the use of mutual observation, sometimes through video recordings (Ainscow, 1999), and evidence collected from students about teaching and learning arrangements within a school (Ainscow & Kaplan, 2006; Messiou, 2006; Miles & Kaplan, 2005). Under certain conditions such approaches provided *interruptions* that stimulated self-questioning, creativity, and action. In so doing, they sometimes led to a reframing of perceived problems that, in turn, drew attention to overlooked possibilities for addressing barriers to participation and learning.

However, none of this provided a straightforward mechanism for the development of more inclusive practices. We found that any space for reflection that was created as a result of engaging with evidence may be filled according to conflicting agendas. Indeed, we documented detailed examples of how deeply held beliefs within schools prevented the experimentation that is necessary in order to foster the development of more inclusive ways of working (Howes & Ainscow, 2006; Ainscow & Kaplan, 2006). This reminds us that it is easy for educational difficulties to be pathologised as difficulties inherent within students. This is why leadership is such a key factor in challenging such assumptions.

We concluded that a methodology for developing inclusive practices must take account of the social processes of learning that go on within particular contexts. From our experience, this requires a group of stakeholders within a particular context to look for a common agenda to guide their discussions of practice and, at much the same time, a series of struggles to establish ways of working that enable them to collect and find meaning in different types of information.

Thinking and Talking. The implication of all of this is that becoming more inclusive is a matter of thinking and talking, reviewing and refining practice, and making attempts to develop a more inclusive culture. Within the network, a key strategy for encouraging this possibility was the development of a programme of school-to-school visits. Many of the staff involved found these occasions both enjoyable and fruitful. We were interested in why this was so and we wanted to explore its potential as a way of sustaining the work of the network.

The visits were not, however, always successful. This seemed to be particularly so when the host teachers interpreted the visits solely as opportunities for the visitors to learn. On these occasions, the hosts positioned themselves as teachers rather than learners. Typically, the visit then consisted of a demonstration or performance of various teaching strategies that had been judged to be successful. On these occasions, those receiving the visit might merely rehearse what they already knew and respond to questions beyond the procedural as if they were challenges, rather than openings for debate.

On the other hand, successful visits were usually characterised by a sense of mutual learning amongst hosts and visitors. It was noticeable, too, that the focus for these visits often took some time to identify and clarify. Indeed, the preliminary negotiations that took place were in themselves a key aspect of the process. So, for example, during one such visit, the visitors were each invited to observe two children. A simple observation framework focussed on children's interactions with peers and teachers. Those to be observed were chosen by the class teacher on the basis that they were the children he/she knew least about in his/her class. In addition to observations, the visiting teachers were asked to interview the children. Again, a loose structure was devised but the main emphasis was on the visiting teachers following up things that they had seen during observations.

Afterwards, one of the visiting teachers said that the day had been 'absolutely fascinating'. He added, 'There is no way in your own school you could do this'. The host head teacher commented more specifically on the interviews that the visitors had carried out with pupils: 'It's so different to what they're like in the school... pupils say things to outsiders that they just wouldn't say to us'. This seemed to be born out by some of the imagery used by pupils about their teachers in interviews that day. For example, one commented: 'He's like a piranha looking round the class. He knows when I'm not listening'. Another pupil remarked: 'He could be a really good teacher if he could explain, but he gets too frustrated.' The joking response by the class teacher to such statements was: 'I want to go home! I've had enough now!'

The personal nature of these observations, and the teacher's willingness to listen to this feedback with colleagues from his/her own and another school, illustrate the extent of the challenge that was sometimes involved in this sort of collaboration. Indeed, our experience was that such visits were neither 'cosy', nor did they always result in a rosy glow. The key factor seemed to be that of mutual challenge and this is, we believe, more likely under the sorts of conditions I have outlined.

In deriving lessons from this example, it is important to emphasise the variety of reasons why participants were able to frame the event as one from which everyone might learn. This was connected to the fact that the evidence that was generated, and the ways in which it was responded to, opened up further questions. The participants also had the time necessary, not just for the event itself, but for formulating the agenda for the visit and for quite lengthy discussion afterwards. Further, they had a wider forum—the LEA network meetings—in which they felt comfortable enough to talk about quite 'risky' findings. In this forum they knew they had established the sorts of relationships where others were more likely to congratulate them on their work and be intrigued by what had happened, rather than to pass judgments. The atmosphere and nature of the network meetings, by this point, was significantly different from earlier meetings. They were much more open ended, there was much more unstructured conversation, and there was a sense that people felt they were 'amongst friends'. This allowed different sorts of exchanges to take place, whereby the participants felt able to 'think aloud', trying to make sense of what had happened as a consequence of their involvement in the network.

In summary, then, the work of the Tramton inclusion network, over 3 years, demonstrated the power of using evidence to stimulate collaboration between practitioners within a school, and with colleagues in partner schools. These experiences suggest that successful collaboration involves a complex social process within which colleagues with very different experiences, beliefs and assumptions learn how to learn from these differences. The problem was, however, that the network only involved nine schools and, as a result, remained a somewhat fragile initiative within the local authority.

8.5 Phase 3 (2004–2007)—Networking Across the Authority

Building on the lessons of these earlier experiences, the Tramton local authority went on to develop an ambitious strategy for involving all schools in processes of networking. This involved the creation of a network involving all of the authority's secondary schools, and eight networks that included all 58 of its primary schools. In what follows the focus is on our analysis of what happened in the primary sector.

Establishing Networks. The assumption was that strengthening processes of networking would help to spread good practice and share resources in ways that could create greater equity across the system. This echoed the findings of the Phase 2 network and, indeed, our research elsewhere (Ainscow, Muijs, & West, 2006; Ainscow & West, 2006; Ainscow & Howes, 2007). However, the setting up of the new primary networks proved to be a complex business that led to a degree of tension between local authority staff and some head teachers.

Whilst there are a few schools in the authority that serve 'middle class' communities, the majority cater for children from economically poorer backgrounds. Usually schools serve either mostly Asian heritage or mostly White populations, with just a few having a more mixed intake. Self selection by heads themselves was the starting point for some of the groupings, other arrangements also occurred and for a few schools the reason they were in a particular network was that, simply put, they were the ones that were left behind.

Because of these various factors, the eight networks were noticeably different in make up. Some were geographically very close, serving schools with similar neighbourhoods; others were much more diverse and included schools from different parts of the authority. There are many faith schools in the area and some of the networks had a preponderance of church schools, whilst others had none. There was also fluidity between the networks, with schools leaving one to join another. In addition, there was some manipulation on the part of local authority officers, where, because of particular circumstances or concerns, a school was allocated to a network.

Collecting Evidence. Our involvement began in the summer of 2005 and was seen as a process of evaluation.[3] Data were collected using a mix of methods: regular

[3]The third phase was an authority commissioned evaluation I carried out with Anne Francis.

meetings with SIOs; observations of meetings and staff development events; analysis of various policy documents; a questionnaire survey of representatives of each of the eight networks; and interviews with key individuals in schools, the local authority and the various support agencies. Towards the end of the 2-year period, in the summer of 2007, process and outcome data were analysed and compared with a view to determining conclusions as to the effectiveness of the initiative. These findings were validated with stakeholders groups and then used to encourage processes of reflection amongst senior staff in schools and the LEA.

We found that the degree of involvement within schools and networks varied considerably. The evidence indicated that it was head teachers, in the main, who had the power to make a network successful. Where they were committed to putting time aside to attend meetings and to enable staff to be fully involved, the network developed. So, for example, the heads in one network met once a fortnight, leading a SIO to comment: 'Heads aren't going to commit to this level of time unless it is worthwhile'. Other groups of heads met monthly or half-termly, and many were also in regular email contact. For some, it seems, this became one of the most important aspects of their professional lives. A SIO commented: 'If the death of the isolation of head teachers is achieved, it will be a very significant development, creating the capacity for change and development'.

Apart from senior staff, members of staff designated as 'lead learners' were often the group most involved. Usually they were at the forefront of curriculum developments, meeting with colleagues from other schools regularly, and leading developments in their own school. Such opportunities to try things out and report findings back to the working group appeared to provide a very powerful form of professional development. One young teacher commented, 'It's one of the best things that has happened to me'. An experienced teacher described how four of her lead learner colleagues, at her invitation, came to observe a numeracy lesson; they focussed on four children the teacher was concerned about, carrying out a detailed observation and interviewing the children after the lesson. Their feedback was enormously helpful, said the teacher, and led to significant changes in practice; for example, one child told the observer that he could not do things quickly enough in his head and would like to write things down—the teacher therefore provided all children with whiteboards from then on.

Areas of Focus. For most networks the core purpose was that of teaching and learning. However, two networks were asked by the local authority to explore ways of integrating the role of different external children's support agencies, including those from the health and social services. For some this complexity muddied the waters. 'We lost our way', said one head, 'but now we have gone back and agreed that our aim is raising standards'.

Through the power they gained together, some networks began to renegotiate their relationship with the local authority. As a result, heads began to decide when and how they wanted to do things; for example, one group organised their own training for the government's new primary strategy, informing the local authority what they wanted from them, rather than waiting to be invited to the training the authority was planning.

Many head teachers found the networks so powerful that they said that they intended to continue working in this way even if there was no additional funding made available.

Drawing Out the Lessons. Reflecting further on the evidence we collected over 2 years points to some potentially important lessons. What occurred has to be understood as eight separate cases, each set within the wider context of the case of the local authority. All of this, in turn, has to be understood against the backcloth of the on-going changes in national policy. Inevitably, therefore, the processes and outcomes varied between the different networks.

In the most promising examples, we saw evidence of considerable progress towards school-to-school partnerships that had a significant impact on policy and practice. Here it is tempting to look for patterns in order to make generalisations as to what actions are needed to develop an effective network. However, any such conclusions must be seen as being tentative, to say the least. In terms of geography and the patterns of involvement, for example, we saw cases where a district-based approach, with relatively homogeneous groups of schools had certain advantages. On the other hand, elsewhere we heard a strong case made for cross-district arrangements that bring together schools serving different contexts and pupil populations in a way that seemed to encourage learning from difference.

In some cases, historical factors played a part. As I have explained, some groupings built on successful experiences in relation to earlier projects. In some cases, too, established friendship groups amongst heads formed the basis for the creation of a network. There are, however, dangers in such arrangements as far as equity is concerned, not least when some schools are excluded.

Across the eight accounts we saw evidence of the key roles of individuals, particularly in the early setting up phases of a network. However, progress seemed to be strongly associated with a sense of shared leadership, particularly amongst heads and other senior staff. Such an approach seemed to emerge over time, as relationships deepen and trust grows. Being prepared to reveal worries about your own school is potentially threatening within an education service which is so dominated by competition. In a number of the networks, staff visited one another's schools in ways that draws back the veil of secrecy. At the same time, some of the groups began to learn the potential power of sharing data and using external colleagues as critical friends in relation to drawing out implications for further improvement efforts.

All of this points to one of the key challenges: that of finding time. Whilst having access to additional resources is clearly very helpful in this respect, it was evident that where a group of heads experienced the benefits of collaboration, they were prepared to make strategic decisions to release human resources in order to invest in the strengthening of their partnerships. This reminds us that, as far as schools are concerned, time is the currency used to indicate that something is of importance. In other words, there is no extra time but if we see something as being a priority, we find the time.

In this sense, attitudes and beliefs are important factors. It is noticeable, for example, that during the early stages the idea of setting up networks was met with a degree of understandable cynicism. In a few of the networks this was not fully overcome, particularly amongst senior staff.

Progress seemed to be associated with activities around agendas that were determined by schools and that were seen to have the potential to make direct contributions to the core business of teaching and learning. This seemed to create a common sense of purpose and, indeed, a common process for implementation that encouraged the sharing of expertise. The idea of setting up lead teachers to coordinate implementation efforts proved to be particularly effective and the linking of these staff across schools clearly added considerable value to the process.

Joint staff development events were particularly well received in many of the schools. Then, more specifically, support for schools in difficulty and the mentoring of newly appointed heads proved to be powerful processes. Indeed it became increasingly apparent that, in the most mature networks, schools were increasingly looking to one another for advice and support. Inevitably, this has implications for the future roles of local authority staff.

Processes of networking remained fluid, as individual schools felt that it was to their benefit to belong to different groupings for different purposes. We also saw how, occasionally, a school may choose to move from one network to another. In this sense, it is better to think of networking as a process, rather than as a fixed state. Presumably, then, a feature of an effective local authority would be its capacity to orchestrate networking in order to make good use of all the available expertise to the benefit of all of its children. All of this points to potentially important roles for authority officers in fostering, monitoring, and brokering such processes.

Tensions and Uncertainties. Despite the impressive progress that was made in most of the networks, the processes involved continued to be fraught with uncertainties, not least because of an absence of overall policy direction. Consequently, they remained fragile. All of this throws light on the way national policies, as they are interpreted at the local authority level, impact on the actions of schools.

Throughout the 2 years, we noted examples of how these uncertainties played out on the ground, leading to a lack of overall coherence, as those in schools sensed they were receiving competing and, sometimes, contradictory messages as to where they should place their priorities. This was most striking in terms of the continuing tensions between strategies for raising standards, as measured in terms of test and examination scores, and measures taken in relation to notions of social justice and inclusion, with the focus on those learners who remain marginalised despite the efforts made to raise standards.

So, for example, we saw how the two networks that were asked to explore multiagency working were pulled in different directions. Early on they were encouraged by local authority colleagues to take on an 'assessment for learning' initiative. Then, at a later stage, pressure was put on the two networks to attend training days regarding the idea of 'extended schools'. These and other initiatives are, of course, all in their own way important. However, as I have already noted, the success of the networks appeared to come from the sense of commitment that occurs when they determine their own improvement agendas. This being the case, it was hardly surprising when some networks started to resist what they saw as 'high jacking' of the agenda by the local authority.

In fairness, it is important to note that local authority officers act in the context of pressures (and, sometimes, opportunities) that are created by national agencies. On the other hand, a key role for the local authority must be to create a sense of overall coherence and direction, by drawing staff and partners together around a common mission. More specifically, its aim should be to articulate a clear vision of what the education service should look like that can focus improvement efforts, leaving the networks themselves to generate their own specific goals in relationship to this vision. In this way, I suggest, the tensions that occurred as some networks grew in strength would be much less likely and the power of networking mobilised.

Impact. The experience of these eight networks adds to the growing body of evidence which suggests that processes of networking can strengthen the capacity of schools to respond to learner diversity. Whilst the results were uneven and the progress remained fragile, the evidence was that in Tramton, school-to-school collaboration led to:

- Improvements in teaching and learning
- Powerful forms of professional development at all levels, not least that of head teachers
- A greater capacity for managing change and implementing innovations
- Effective induction of newly appointed head teachers
- The creation of a more cooperative environment within which external support staff, including those from other agencies, can work more effectively

All of this occurred through the negotiation of new working relationships within schools and between schools, and between groups of schools and external partners. In the most promising examples, this involved the strengthening of 'social capital' in ways described by Hargreaves, A., (2003a), such that available expertise was being used more effectively to serve a wider population of learners than is possible when human resources are trapped within the walls of individual institutions.

8.6 Some Implications

The findings of the 10-year programme of development and research in Tramton do not provide a simple formula that can be used by education systems as they try to develop ways of working that will achieve both excellence and equity. Rather they suggest a series of propositions around which future actions might be planned. In summary, these are as follows:

- *Schools know more than they use*—Thus the main thrust of development has to be with making better use of existing expertise and creativity within all the member organisations in a local area.

- *The expertise of teachers and educational leaders is largely unarticulated*—Therefore, in order to access the reservoir of unused expertise, it is necessary to create a common language of practice that will facilitate mutual reflection and the sharing of ideas.
- *Evidence is the engine for change*—Specifically, it can help to create space for re-appraisal and re-thinking by interrupting existing discourses, and by focussing attention on overlooked possibilities for moving practice forward.
- *Networking is socially complex*—Successful networking requires new thinking and, indeed, new relationships at the systems level that foster active connections amongst stakeholders.
- *Leadership must foster inter-dependence*—There is a need for forms of leadership that encourage the trust, mutual understanding, and shared values and behaviours, that will bind members of a network together and make cooperative action possible.

These ideas have implications for what needs to happen within networks of schools, across district education systems, and at the national level.

At *the network level*, we saw how the networking between schools that took place in Tramton varied from context to context. This seems inevitable in that such forms of collaboration involve social learning processes, shaped by particular circumstances, related to history and geography, challenges and opportunities. Here we note echoes of other research into factors influencing the transfer of practice between teachers (Bragg et al., 2004). This suggests that teacher learning is a social process that is sustained by relationships and trust; that it is a personal and inter-personal process that has to engage with teacher and institutional identity; that this requires conditions that provide support for learner engagement and a willingness to try something out; and, lastly, that the work of transfer has to be sustained over time.

It follows that there can be no one recipe for fostering effective networking. On the other hand, certain ingredients seem to be important. These are to do with:

- *Ownership*—In the contexts where collaboration appeared to pay off, it was evident that those in the partner schools—particularly the head teachers—felt that they had reasonable control over the agendas that were to be the focus of the activities.
- *Levels of involvement*—Whilst the commitment of heads and other senior staff is essential, best practice seemed to involve forms of collaboration that existed at many levels within schools.
- *Practical focus*—Focussing on real world issues, particularly those to do with the core business of teaching and learning, seemed to provide the best type of vehicle for learning how to work together effectively.
- *Making time*—Since successful collaboration demands an investment of people's time and energy, it is hardly surprising that good practice was associated with flexible management arrangements that provided staff with opportunities to learn from one another

- *Commitment to values*—In those networks that seem to be maturing into forms of collaboration that looked to be potentially more sustainable, the focus moved from attention to specific projects towards a deeper level of partnership around common beliefs and values.
- *Shared responsibility*—Successful networking leads to changes in organisational cultures and, therefore, demands the sharing of responsibility through new forms of collaborative leadership.

Alongside our experiences of school-toschool collaboration in other settings, the developments in Tramton led us to formulate a model for analysing forms of networking within particular contexts in order to move thinking and practice forward (Chapman & Ainscow, 2007). It takes the form of a *framework for networking* consisting of four interlinked elements, each with its own set of issues for consideration, as follows:

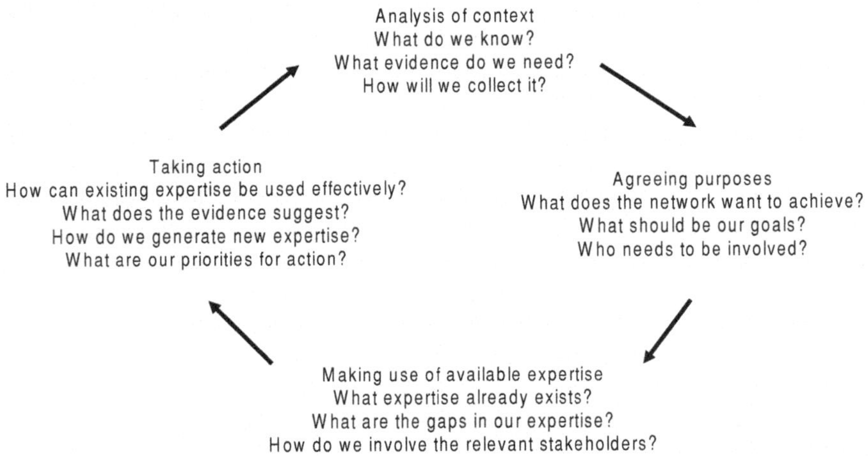

The framework pinpoints guiding questions that can be used by those involved in initiating and strengthening networks to develop a greater understanding of their own contexts, and their associated processes and practices. Its use requires the development of leadership that will encourage action and shared responsibility at all levels of the system. And, with regard to children's learning experiences, the classroom level is seen as being crucial, since, as became clear in Tramton, teachers *are* decision makers and, therefore, policy makers.

Changing policy and practice at the classroom level is particularly difficult, however, in that it most often requires changes in thinking and beliefs. As we have seen, in more mature networks, engaging with evidence of various kinds can be a powerful means of encouraging professional dialogue that can stimulate the sharing of expertise amongst practitioners. Specifically, it can help to create space for reappraisal and rethinking, by interrupting existing discourses, and by focussing attention on overlooked possibilities for moving practice forward.

Moving to *implications at that district level*, the changes that occurred in Tramton began to redesign what is meant by the local authority. This involved a move away from the traditional 'them and us' relationship between central office staff and schools, to one of shared responsibility. It involved working together to make use of the pressure for change stemming from national policies, whilst mobilising available human resources at the local level around a common sense of purpose. This is most likely to be achieved when local leadership makes connections between national policies and local priorities. It also means that there is a need to create locally the organisational conditions and climate within which stakeholders will feel encouraged to work together creatively to invent new and more effective responses to old problems—especially those of learners who are not making satisfactory progress.

The emphasis on school level leadership, within a change model grounded in the notion that a combination of robust national policies and strong school management is the surest way to bring about improvements in teaching and learning, has very significant implications for the roles of local authority staff. It means that they have to adjust their priorities and ways of working in response to the development of collaborative arrangements that are led from within schools. And, as we have seen, at a time when they too are under increasing pressure to deliver improvements in results across their stocks of schools, this can sometimes lead to misunderstandings and tensions between senior staff in schools and their local authority partners.

Despite such difficulties, I cannot conceive of a way for collaboration to continue as a central element of effective school improvement strategies, without some form of local co-ordination. As I have indicated, the contributions of local authority staff were significant in the development of collaborative arrangements in Tramton. Specifically, local authority staff had a key role in supporting and challenging schools in relation to the agreed goals of collaborative activities, whilst head teachers shared responsibility for the overall management of improvement efforts within their schools.

This distinction sharpens understanding of the sorts of roles that local authority staff need to take on: *not* managing and leading change, but rather working in partnership with senior people in schools to strengthen collaborative ways of working. In such contexts they can ensure that specific challenges which derive from their knowledge of the bigger picture across the authority are addressed, and also contribute to the clarity of purpose and practical working arrangements, as well as playing an important role in the monitoring and evaluation of progress. At the same time, they can help to broker the sharing of resources and expertise. However, the changes in attitude and practice that this implies are likely to be challenging to the existing thinking of many experienced local authority staff.

Finally, this analysis has *implications for national policy makers*. If they see school networking as a means of achieving both excellence and equity, they will need to foster greater flexibility at the local level in order that practitioners have the space to analyse their local circumstances and determine priorities accordingly. If that happens, the potential for developments such as those going on in Tramton to grow will be much greater.

Chapter 9
Widening Opportunities? A Case Study of School-to-School Collaboration in a Rural District

9.1 Introduction

Most research on networking and collaboration to date has focussed on schools serving disadvantaged urban communities that may face severe pressure from accountability systems demanding improved performance, but little attention has so far been paid to collaboration between schools in rural areas, not least due to views of a 'rural idyll' where strong prosperous communities support local schools (Cloke, 2003). Indeed, rural communities tend to be more socially cohesive than many or their urban counterparts and, in England, do not face the challenges of social disadvantage seen in many of our inner cities (though rural areas do, of course, encompass sites of considerable disadvantage). However, while not usually facing the same levels of social disadvantage that urban schools do (though there are of course disadvantaged rural areas in many parts of England), rural schools confront some specific challenges, such as limited aspirations, with rural youth often perceiving less of a relationship between education and work than urban youth, and exhibiting a stronger attachment to place that makes them less keen to move to higher education institutions that are often in larger cities removed from their area (Kannappel & DeYoung, 1999). Rural youth are less likely to participate in post-compulsory education and training than urban youth, when cancelling out the impact of socio-economic status, though there is some evidence that increased provision of vocational pathways can lead to greater post-compulsory participation (Abbott-Chapman, & Kilpatrick, 2001; Lamb & Rumberger, 1999, Johns, Kilpatrick, & Loechel, 2003) A feeling of disconnection and anomie are often present due to remoteness from central LEA systems and from alternative centres of expertise such as higher education institutions, which is amplified by the imposition of central government policies that are often geared towards urban issues and take little account of the specificity of rural contexts (Kannappel & DeYoung, 1999). In small schools, accountability measures can be particularly problematic and alienating, due to the susceptibility of results to the performance of a limited number of pupils (Linn et al., 2002). Where rural areas face exurbanisation or suburbanisation, they often face additional forces of disconnect due to the divide between indigenous inhabitants and newcomers, and schools often end up playing a much less central role in the community than heretofore (Howley et al., 2005). The remoteness of rural schools from central services

D. Muijs et al., *Collaboration and Networking in Education*,
DOI 10.1007/978-94-007-0283-7_9, © Springer Science+Business Media B.V. 2011

can be a particular problem when addressing issues of inclusion, as the often small schools may lack the resources (trained staff, materials, funding) to address the special needs of particular (groups of) pupils (Sze, 2004). Some studies suggest that professional development can be less developed in some rural areas due to remoteness from central services and lack of resources (Howley et al., 2005). Of course, the category of rural schools is in itself problematic, with rural areas ranging from exurbanised prosperity to impoverished former coalfield areas, so any generalisation must be treated cautiously.

Because of these rural issues, some of the advantages of collaboration may be particularly strong for schools serving rural districts, where the ability to provide a wide curriculum and opportunities for all students, including those with special needs, may be limited.

In England, initiatives promoting collaboration in rural schools have attempted to address some of the scale issues confronted by them. For example, in the 1980s Education Support Grants were used to promote the forming of clusters of rural primary schools, in a programme known as the Rural Schools Curriculum Enhancement (Hall & Wallace, 1993). The evaluation of this project suggested that schools in collaborative clusters experienced less anxiety and difficulties in implementing the new National Curriculum than schools that were not part of a cluster (Hargreaves, Comer, & Galton, 1996). Other studies point to the ability to provide stronger provision for pupils with SEN thanks to sharing of resources (Norwich, Evans, Lunt, Steedman, & Wedell, 1994). Collaboration in rural districts was also stimulated by the Technical & Vocational Education Initiative (TVEI). Studies on rural schools within this programme point to small rural schools seeing collaboration as being able to help solve particular issues caused by their often small size (Busher & Hodgkinson, 1996). Therefore, evidence of, in particular, the benefits of collaboration to rural schools in terms of the sharing of resources and the sharing of experiences is evident here.

However, research in disadvantaged urban contexts still dominates studies into collaboration (as is evident from, suggest that collaboration can aid school improvement in these context both through overcoming anomie, contributing to direct impact activities such as sharing key staff at moments of crisis, building capacity, for example through joint CPD, sustaining improvement, through pooling resources and leadership, and sharing leadership. Furthermore, it has been posited that networks lead to more equitable forms of school improvement, in that by collaboratively focussing on an area they can lessen the negative impact of competition and improvement of individual schools, which may be at the expense of other schools, and thus pupils, in the area (Ainscow & West, 2006). In this paper we will use a case study approach to explore these issues in a rural, and more socio-economically advantaged context. Thus, can collaboration address similar issues as found in urban contexts in terms of short and long-term improvement and equity, what are the contextual factors that specifically impact on these rural schools, and does collaboration, as suggested earlier, have a specific role in school improvement in rural contexts?

9.2 Context and Methods

A qualitative case study methodology was employed to look at the case of a rural federation of schools, formed in an English county. Federations are collaborative networks of schools enjoying legal status and some additional funding from the government. Federations are more or less 'hard', in the sense of having or not having a joint legally constituted governing body and in many cases an executive head teacher responsible for the entire federation. The federation studied here consisted of 10 schools in a rural Local Authority (LA) in England. The local FE college is also part of the federation. Schools are diverse in terms of geographical area and size, ranging from very small rural schools to large semi-urban schools in the larger villages closest to the Motorway. The area is situated in a large rural county. This area is the most affluent in the county, as, whereas many parts of the country are agricultural, and suffering the problems, of the agricultural economy, and others are characterised by declining small scale industries, this area has largely made the transition form agriculture to tourism. In particular, those areas closest to transport hubs have prospered, and have seen an influx of commuters, though some of the more remote villages tend to have benefited less from the tourism boom, and remain more dependent on agriculture. Of course, a reliance on tourism as the key driver of the economy brings its own problems, such as seasonality and the issue of locals being priced out of the housing market.

The federation is best described as a 'soft' federation, not having constituted a joint governing body. However, elements of a 'hard' federation do exist, in that a company was set up to which certain powers have been devolved. The federation decided to develop legal status by setting itself up as a limited company with a joint governing body. An executive group of head teachers became the board of the limited company and the governors meet as a scrutiny committee as members of the company, in order to get them involved, but without the binding legal power of a 'hard' federation.

Case study visits were undertaken to the federation, during which interviews were undertaken with the federation coordinator, head teachers, school governors, teachers, senior managers, and middle managers. Interviews were undertaken with between 4 and 8 staff members in each school, depending on availability of staff for interview, which was largely a function of the size of the school. In all schools the head, at least one member of middle management, and at least one classroom teacher was included in this group. Group interviews were undertaken with pupils in three schools. In one school, one group of Key Stage 3 pupils was interviewed. In a second school a group of Key Stage 3 and a group of Key Stage 4 pupils were interviewed, a group of Key Stage 4 and a group of Key Stage 5 pupils were interviewed, while in the final school a group of Key Stage 5 pupils were interviewed. Groups ranged in size from 4 to 10. Access issues meant that we were somewhat reliant on the schools in terms of the selection of the interviewees, which means that representativeness cannot be guaranteed. Documentary evidence, such as federation plans and meeting minutes were analysed, and three meetings were attended, one of the Federation Heads, one of the Company board, and one of a sub-committee. However, while several organisations (school, college) are involved, the study was conceived as a single case study, with the federation as the unit of analysis, in view of the fact that our focus was on collaboration and networks, rather than on individual schools. However, obviously differences between and impact on individual schools were scrutinised.

The trustworthiness of the evidence was scrutinised by comparing and contrasting evidence from different people within a particular context (e.g. teachers, support staff, and students). In utilising this framework, it is important to involve as many participants and other stakeholders in the case studies as possible to ensure that the sample reflects the diversity of actors involved in leadership in schools. Therefore, we interviewed a cross section of people involved in the federation (see above). This should enable us to gain rich data on collaborative practices across the federation, and to interrogate differences in perception that may result from roles (e.g. head, teacher), context (e.g. individual schools, or differences between schools and college), and biography (e.g. gender) as well as allowing us to draw out common themes.

The interviews were semi-structured, to enable us to clearly focus on the key research questions while allowing sufficient flexibility to react to relevant emerging data.

The evidence for was analysed thematically with a view towards determining possible links between contextual factors and collaborative practices and using a coding system corresponding to emerging themes (Miles & Huberman, 1994). An audit trail was created in order that claims about could be subjected to scrutiny (Schwandt & Halpern, 1988). A report based on this analysis was presented to the federation so that those involved had an opportunity to reflect on the findings and to offer comments (Lincoln & Guba, 1985).

9.3 Results

9.3.1 Set-up and Structures

The federation serves an affluent rural area. *People want to live in this area* (head of governing body large school). The good transport infrastructure means that commuting from this attractive area to urban centres is relatively easy. Parents are generally seen as supportive.

The federation was a bottom-up initiative, set up on the urging of heads. Two heads in particular, the heads of the two largest schools in the area, took the lead in setting up and leading the federation, partly as for the smaller schools capacity issues mean that their potential to take the lead in the federation is limited. A small collection of people with a vision have driven the process. *It is essentially personality driven* (head, secondary). New appointments from outside the area to headship in a number of schools was seen as having helped in terms of getting a group of people together who were very keen on giving and receiving mutual support. Governors were not directly involved in setting up the federation, and generally appeared to be less involved in the running of it than heads.

On the ground, the federation operates through a system of working parties. A number of working parties existed focussing on different areas, such as assessment, where different approaches are trialled in one school and shared with others, a 14–19 curriculum group that was working on developing coordinated programmes for this age group across schools, and a data sharing group.

The federation was specifically set up to address perceived challenges of working in a rural area in a large county. The need for some formal collaborative arrangement was seen by one deputy head as greater in this rural and somewhat remote area: *I come from the South East, where everything is close together; London is just down the road. We don't have that here, things are not on hand, so it is important for us to develop collaboration between ourselves, and make sure head teachers meet as a group.* However, she also felt that the federation had actually gone further than the collaboration she experienced in the South East. *In county X we used to work for our schools, but met and chatted regularly to people from other schools. Here we don't just work for our schools, but for the federation as well, and that is an additional aspect I think. You feel you are responsible to and accountable for the federation. It's a bit like being in a department. In (my previous county) we used to, I won't say hide things, but we were in competition.* The size and diversity of the county makes it hard for any collaborative arrangement to be county wide, so the formation of smaller collaboratives appears essential.

Two main issues were seen as challenges in this context. The Local Education Authority was perceived as distant and unconcerned with this area, focussing its efforts on more disadvantaged parts of the county. Also, while the area is generally seen as representing the rural idyll, there are problems with the aspirations of young people in the area, who are able to gain employment in the tourism industry, which while lucrative from the point of view of a teenager offers limited prospects of advancement. There was also a perception that the schools were not able to offer a sufficiently broad curriculum, and were not engaging with the needs of the local economy.

As mentioned above, leadership of the federation rests very much with the head teachers. Governors have been a help in identifying specific issues such as emphasising the need for proper budgeting, but the heads are clearly in control. This dominance of the process by the heads is seen as a key factor in developing the openness that has led to successful collaboration. This means the process is driven forward and led from the top.

As mentioned earlier, the federation is not just dominated by heads, but specifically by the heads of the larger schools, seen as having more capacity to engage in the leadership of the federation as well as having been the drivers towards setting it up in the first place. Getting people comfortable with the notion that the larger schools lead the federation had been a challenge, according to the head of one of the large schools: *There is a need for endless sensitivity with regards to the feelings of others, especially when there are a large number of government initiatives that actually make collaboration quite a difficult thing*. The smaller schools sometimes perceived the federation as being the larger schools telling them what to do, though according to the deputy head of one of the larger school this has improved over time as the smaller schools have gotten to know the working model of the federation. The cultural change required for these feelings to disappear is slow, however. In some of the smaller schools there was still a suspicion that some of the activities of the federation might be aimed primarily at furthering the interests of these large schools: *When I see some policy documents written by certain heads in the federation I do wonder what the motivation is* (governor, smaller school). Schools also have different needs and communities, with some being very rural to some being semi-suburban. According to one head: *The situation of the schools means that they are quite disparate. They are less likely than urban schools to be serving people from the same community*. Distance is an issue here, especially where joint courses are timetabled, as it can be hard for schools to get their pupils to the venue. This can also be a problem in setting up staff meetings in the federation. For small schools in particular, it can be hard for staff to free up time for this.

The federation has also made a number of common appointments. These joint appointments, though still limited in number, were varied in type, from the federation coordinator to a peripatetic chef who goes from school to school organising the catering courses, consultants and working group leaders (e.g. a curriculum extension coordinator in charge of supporting pupils who were 'not best suited for mainstream provision'). In some cases they were secondments from federation schools, in others they were externals from other LAs. Use was made of external consultants to help overcome the fact that capacity to provide services is not always present in a rural area. However, this had been done at a financial cost, and in some cases could hinder integration of federation activities into daily routines of schools, who tended to rely on this external support rather than developing internal capacity. Appointing these shared consultants was something the federation has been able to do that wouldn't have been possible without it. *The financial support for the federation has been very helpful, as it allowed making a number of strategic appointments such as an executive officer to help run the federation smoothly. Even though it is not a massive amount of money, it was enough to allow us to make appointments and get over the problem of schools saying I don't have any money to put in the pot* (head).

The federations programme has therefore been key to developing collaboration in this area. While collaboration existed before the federation, federating has changed the extent of collaboration by creating new systems and structures which would otherwise not have been possible.

9.3.2 Building Relationships

A key issue in getting the federation to work successfully was building up trust and relationships. While the federation could, up to an extent, build on existing relationships in this respect, as some collaboration was evident going back to the

TVEI programme in the 1980s, the deepened relationships that were desired in the federation required careful development. Building trust had been hard, especially as some schools were competing with one another for students. Relationships had largely been developed through action, in that working groups were formed that had brought not just senior leaders and heads but middle managers together, thus developing the ties that can generate trust and collaborative working relationships, especially were the working group was seen to have had positive impact.

While working groups typically consisted of middle managers, increasingly teachers and support staff had been getting together as well. A federation-wide training day was held which was seen as powerful in bringing different groups together *because very rarely do you get the opportunity to meet whole departments from other schools. Not everything will work in your school, but you can adapt things* (head, secondary school). Groups of teachers were increasingly working together as a result of this. This did not mean that everyone in the school was really aware of the federation as most collaboration still occurred either between heads or in the working groups, which were largely made up of middle and senior managers. The fact that not all staff have yet been heavily involved meant that not all the staff in the schools were as enthusiastic about Federating as the heads.

Federation activities done in the working groups were then typically disseminated to staff by middle managers. *Good practice will be cascaded down through middle managers, so in that way everyone is affected* (deputy head). This was not seen as unproblematic, however: *I still think there is a gap between being told about it and actually seeing what happens* (deputy head).

Youngsters themselves were also increasingly working together, which had broken down some of the prejudices that existed between different villages. However, this collaboration at pupil level was still limited to specific groups of pupils, and did not happen across the board.

As well as through action, specific activities had been undertaken to build trust. The main example of this was a joint heads visit to Chile, which, according to the chair of a governing body as well as a deputy head of one school has been very important in making them feel like a group. *Trust, respect, and open communication are the key things for the federation to work* (deputy head). Obviously, tensions did arise, and the role of the federation consultant, an external appointment to the federation not connected to any school in the area, appeared crucial in resolving these through extensive discussion and site visits. An example of how tensions were defused is that when the budget was set up, one school head was more reluctant and had some concerns, so he was put on the budget committee which he normally would not have been a part of. *Essentially, though, it is a case of a lot of discussion, and giving it time, if you don't the wheels can quickly come of the wagon. There is a kind of subtlety involved here* (external consultant).

In a competitive environment, the federation allowed schools to offer support across distance. This made collaboration easier as close proximal schools may see each other as competitors more than schools which are further away. The geographical spread of the federation was an advantage in this respect.

9.3.3 Impact

Participants generally see the federation as having been beneficial to the schools involved. In particular, what the federation had allowed schools to do was to offer a broader curriculum. Expensive vocational options, which had been beyond the resources of individual schools, could now be offered jointly, in part through collaboration with local businesses. Students perceived this change very positively.

A key goal of the federation had been to increase curricular provision in 14–19 in collaboration with the local FE college. Interviewees mentioned this area as a particular success of the federation. *We now have structures in place that mean that all pupils can find an appropriate course. Also for the lower achievers, they can now find pretty convincing provision* (head, large secondary). Key examples of this were joint catering courses, for which a peripatetic chef was appointed, joint health and social work and health and beauty courses, all in collaboration with the college. These courses typically involved 1 day a week spent out of school, at the college or in work settings. This provision was seen to have motivated previously underserved groups of students, improving their attitudes to school. Pupils enjoyed the joint courses with the college, where they felt they were treated more like adults than at school. The professional materials used were also seen by pupils as better than those used in the schools before federating, something that was corroborated by staff who pointed to the opportunities collaboration had provided for developing a more 'realistic' standard of vocational education through use or simulation of actual professional settings. Other programmes, such as joint provision for gifted and talented students, had also come about as a result of the federation.

The federation was seen as being key to the development of these courses: *It would be far harder to manage and put together these programmes without the federation* (head, small school). *We are medium-sized, so when it comes to provision for specific groups such as gifted and talented, we do not have enough pupils. The federation could make a big difference here* (head).

Collaborative approaches had also been successful in developing programmmes for disaffected pupils. Individual schools had previously spent a lot of time dealing with these pupils, as the county did not have the level of alternative provision found in urban areas. A joint approach had allowed alternative provision to be provided to all schools, both through brokering existing provision and through developing new provision. The federation is seen as having been key to this according to the coordinator: *I would say that even 6 months ago we would not have been able to go this far down that road. The trust that has been built has made this possible.* The federation had also benefited from its association with the EBD school, through using their expertise, *rather than as a conduit through which our troubled pupils are passed* (head, secondary school).

As well as allowing the offer of a wider curriculum, the federation also allowed schools to organise or buy in to joint CPD provision. This was seen by most as an improvement on provision offered by the LEA, which was seen as unconcerned about this group of schools.

While these advantages were extolled, there was no evidence that the federation had improved student exam results, which remained static. *It would not look terribly impressive, but at the moment we are still building structures and processes which aim to improve this over the long term* (head). The federation feels that the DfES has unrealistic expectations in this respect, especially with regard the timescale in which improvement is expected to happen. Another head, however, attributes this lack of progress in achievement to *a certain complacency in certain schools around performance* which had led to the federation not concentrating on issues of teaching and learning sufficiently. Furthermore, while the larger schools dominating the federation felt that it was achieving its aims, some of the smaller and more geographically peripheral schools appeared not to be strongly involved in federation activities, and appeared somewhat suspicious of the motives of the large schools. They felt that federation activity had not benefited them as much as it had the more central schools.

As mentioned earlier, the federation was at least in part an attempt to take over particular local authority functions. For example, the 'Every Child Matters' agenda, which emphasises greater collaboration between schools and other services aimed at children and has led to restructuring of Local Education Authorities into Children's Services departments including social services at the local level, was seen as somewhat problematic in terms of how it had impacted on the LA and its relations with the schools. *Their leadership is struggling because there is a big new agenda out there. The restructuring means they are facing different directions rather than focussing on education.* The federation had in a way moved onto this vacated territory, but the LA felt threatened by this. *We thought that the LA would be happy for us to move onto this vacated territory, but on the contrary they feel threatened by the idea of loosing control. We are a touch disappointed that they haven't just said, you are doing well, but have been rather protective and reluctant. It is a big cultural change.* (federation director). There were tensions with the local authority over a number of specific issues. For example, the federation wanted to employ its ASTs to work within the federation rather than be used LA wide. This was seen as likely to be more effective *LA wide there is a poorly coordinated system, and therefore there is a tendency for head teachers to use ASTs just in their schools. There are some very good people in the county, but quite a few who are not working well for us* (head).

A key sustainability issue is therefore how relations and power structures with the LA will evolve. The federation would like to have more funding delegated from the authority. *The reason is we are a more affluent area, and if we got a per capita share we would be better off than at present. So we would kind of be robbing the poor, if you like, but you can understand our reason for wanting to do it, and as a member of the federation I support that tactic* (head). *Where there are services that we as a federation can do more efficiently, more effectively, than we should be doing that* (head). Clearly, then, the federation can be seen as part of an evolution whereby, as the role of the LA in education has weakened, schools are coming together to create intermediate structures that can take up some of the roles which LAs are no longer able to fulfil effectively. The head of the federation believed that the move, certainly in this LA, is towards more and more provision of services from diverse organisations outwith the central services of the LA. This is seen as a general trend, but one that is particularly strong here due to the diversity of the LA. *It seems likely that the future lies with us taking control of our own area and moving on. We want to get stuff away from the county that we are responsible and accountable for. But at the moment we don't yet have enough structures in place* (deputy head). How the role of the LA within ECM and the role of the federation and similar networks can be reconciled is a key issue, and one that should be an important consideration for national policy.

9.4 Discussion

Overall, then, it would appear that collaboration can have significant benefits for schools in rural areas, through the ability to pool resources to offer a broader curriculum and more CPD opportunities. What was less apparent was the creation of learning communities, as advocated in the literature on collaboration, and no immediate impacts on achievement were reported.

This supports views that see collaboration as having differential impacts in different areas. The view of collaboration as a panacea for school improvement is not supported, and short-term expectations of achievement gains are unlikely to occur in this type of collaborative, consisting of a large number of schools which show reasonable parity in terms of achievement, rather than models where one high-performing school works with a limited number of poorly performing ones. However, impact does appear in the other key areas discussed above, namely capacity building and resource sharing. CPD provision has clearly improved as a result of this collaboration, and the sharing of resources has brought greater opportunity in this area as well as in that of curricular provision. Therefore, some support is provided to conceptual models of school improvement through collaboration, in that aspects such as overcoming anomie, building capacity through joint CPD, and sustaining improvement through pooling resources and leadership (Ainscow & West, 2006), were present in this case study. The study also supports previous research on collaboration in rural contexts, pointing to the value of collaboration in allowing schools to pool resources. There was also some evidence of the value for schools of collaborating with those they perceived as facing similar issues and situations, as found in Busher and Hodgkinson's (1996) earlier study.

Specifically in rural areas, collaboration may help to solve key issues, by pooling resources in a system that tends to target funding at inner city areas, and by allowing schools to develop collaborative structures in areas where local authorities are weak or lack capacity. It is clear that this example of collaboration has addressed some of the issues that rural schools faced. One way it has done this is by providing an organisational structure closer to the schools than the LA, thus somewhat alleviating the distance that exists there. Furthermore, the issue of provision for students with special educational needs is being addressed through the federation, again pointing to potential benefits of collaboration in rural areas. The federation is also attempting to address issues of provision in terms of vocational courses, though whether this will lead to greater participation in HE remains to be seen at this point in time. It would thus appear that collaboration has a number of specific advantages for schools in rural areas.

A number of tensions emerged, however. The first one was the tendency of the federation to replicate on a smaller scale not just some of the activities of the LA, but also some of its problems. Just as the LA was seen as distant and dominated by the more urban and coastal areas, the federation was seen by some of the peripheral schools as dominated by the larger, more central schools. A second tension was that between competition and collaboration, a problem for all collaborative activity taking place in a quasi-marketised system where schools are held individually accountable for results. Having many meetings and joint activities had helped build up trust, and there appeared to be positive relations between heads. However, a measure of distrust still existed regarding the motivation of the leading schools, in particular among governors. The issue of accountability therefore remains particularly problematic for the smaller schools in this area.

The issue of resources can also be problematic. It became clear during interviews and meetings attended that at least part of the motivation behind the federation was in the long run to gain direct control of government funding outwith the LA, which was seen as disadvantaging this group of schools. However, the main reason for lower per capita funding for these schools in comparison with other LA areas was due to the far more disadvantaged intakes of the better funded schools. Different perceptions of equity and fairness underlie arguments in this area, but anyone viewing equity as requiring greater resources for those pupils facing social and economic disadvantage has to be troubled by a system in which the LA coordinating role is replaced by smaller groupings protecting localised interests at the expense of broader issues of equity in the county. It is clear therefore that the view which sees collaboration as necessarily leading to more equitable school improvement is over-optimistic, or overly bound to particular (urban) contexts.

Overall, while this study provides evidence of the benefits of collaboration in rural areas, it also provides a corrective to overly messianic advocates, who idealise collaboration and ignore issues of power and politics that continue to play a key role within networks and in the relationships of networks to their environment and other actors. Furthermore, it is clear that collaboration is contextual, able to fulfil different goals in different contexts. Configurations of collaboration are important here. Large groupings are likely to be helpful in terms of resource sharing, but less so in terms of short-term achievement gains. Larger groupings are also more likely to take on a more confederal structure, where schools retain significant independence, rather than leading to merged governance structures or executive forms of collaborative leadership.

This case study therefore suggests that collaboration can be a useful strategy for rural schools faced with issues such as scarce resources, limited capacity in terms of broadening curricular provision, and remoteness from local authority decision-making centres, but also that the role of LAs may remain crucial in ensuring equity at a broader level.

Chapter 10
Leadership in Full-Service Extended Schools: Communicating Across Cultures

10.1 The Move to Extended Schools

Educational reform tends to operate in cycles, whereby reforms are abandoned and replaced, in many cases to be revisited and revised at a later date, as prior reforms come to be seen as not fully having addressed the key educational issues they set out to remedy (Ravitch, 2000). In particular, the issue of social disadvantage and its relationship to educational outcomes is one that is almost permanently a matter of concern for policy makers, educators, and researchers. Various strategies exist that attempt to improve the educational opportunities of disadvantaged groups. School effectiveness and school improvement have traditionally focused on schools as largely single purpose institutions, devoted to educating children of a particular age and stage of learning, and have aimed to improve within school processes, in particular in those schools serving disadvantaged communities, to this effect (Muijs, 2006b). While many examples can be found in the literature of successful and effective schools serving disadvantaged communities, it is likewise the case that these efforts have not succeeded very well in overcoming social disadvantage, and have left the gap between social classes in terms of achievement largely unaffected (Levin, 2006; Harris, Chapman, Muijs, Russ, & Stoll, 2006). Alongside this emphasis on within-school change, there has for a long time also existed a movement towards strengthening links between schools and communities, that has seen schools as key actors in reaching out to, and collaborating with the community. In England, for example, the Community Schools movement of the 1970s was set up for this purpose (Cummings & Dyson, 2007). Likewise, however, initiatives in countries such as the Netherlands, the US, and Australia have emphasised schools as full-centers for their communities addressing the whole child (Dryfoos, 1995; van Veen, Day, & Walraven, 1998), while recently the English government has likewise moved in that direction with the Full-Service Extended Schools programme. This is seen as especially beneficial where schools are serving disadvantaged areas (Department for Education and Skills, 2003).

D. Muijs et al., *Collaboration and Networking in Education*,

DOI 10.1007/978-94-007-0283-7_10,

Three key premises which underlie this movement are:

- The need to address psychological, health, and social as well as educational issues if students from disadvantaged areas are to reach their full potential;
- The potential power of schools as organisations to reach out to their community; and
- The importance of stronger linkages with the community to improving parental involvement and, as a result of this, student performance (Hiatt-Michael, 2003).

This view is based upon the view that pupils are unlikely to perform to their potential if they suffer from health or social problems, and that therefore addressing these issues is a vital precursor to educational achievement as well as more generally enhancing pupils' life chances and well-being. Furthermore, it is often stated that engaging with other agencies will help the school become more central to the community, thus involving parents more strongly than is currently the case in many disadvantaged communities. This movement has received considerable support in some 'futures scenarios' (e.g. Organisation for Economic Cooperation and Development, 2001).

'Extended schools', or 'full-service' schools are therefore charged with offering or working closely with other agencies that offer, child care, social services, adult education, health services and other forms of provision to pupils and, increasingly, to the community as a whole, alongside their traditional educational role. Different models exist, but all share the fact that school facilities are used for delivering services in partnership with other agencies (Dryfoos, 1995).

The need for more joined-up collaboration between the different agencies working with children is another reason for the formation of extended schools. In England, the Victoria Climbie scandal highlighted the need for multiagency cooperation, and led to the government legislating for interagency work through the 'Every Child Matters' white paper. This was in fact not a freestanding or new policy, but rather the culmination of a move towards multiagency work seen as necessary to help achieve the government's social inclusion agenda, as evidenced in policies such as Sure Start, Education Action Zones, and Connexions, as well as in work outside of education in the areas of domestic violence and sex work, for example (Boynton & Cusick, 2006).

The research evidence for this type of interagency work is mixed. In what is probably the largest study to date, Cummings et al. (forthcoming) report that multiagency work has positive effects on the development of individual pupils and targeted 'at-risk groups' within schools, without necessarily changing the culture of the school or impacting more widely. Similar findings were reported by Cummings and Dyson (2007) in their case study of nine schools in North-East England, where small-scale impacts were found. These results also echo those of the evaluation of the Victorian Full-Service Schools programme in Australia, which was found to have some benefits for students unlikely to stay on at school, while not showing significant wider benefits (James, St Leger, & Ward, 2001).

In an earlier study by Atkinson, Halsey, Kinder, and Wilkin (2002), positive impacts were found in terms of delivering a wider range of services and leading staff involved to have a broader perspective on their work, though increased demands and pressures were also mentioned. Competing priorities and resourcing were mentioned as problems associated with multiagency work. Communication between agency staff was seen as a key challenge. Common aims, commitment, and clear structures needed to be in place for the work to be successful. In particular, agencies and staff needed to want to be involved and be committed to multiagency work, rather than be coerced into it. In a review on the literature on supporting children in special circumstances, Statham (2004) found multiagency work that addressed the whole child rather than compartmentalising services to be characteristic of the most promising approaches, as were links between adult and children's services. Similar findings were reported by Dryfoos (1995) in an earlier US study. Warmington (2004) warn of a lack of fit between traditional structures and cultures and models of interagency work, and highlight the need for professional learning to take place before multiagency work can be effective.

One aspect of extended schools that has not been frequently studied is leadership, even though it is on occasion mentioned as a key factor to effective collaboration (e.g. Raham, 1998). Specific research on leadership in extended schools is rare, though there is some evidence of the leadership challenges in extant literature, such as the need for careful planning and preparation for setting up the necessary collaborative arrangements (Dryfoos, 1995), as well as the emphasis on common aims, which would point us to the role of leaders, instrumental as they are in goal-setting in schools (Leithwood, 1992). Another challenge that arises where different agencies collaborate is that of power and influence. School heads will sometimes assume that the power they enjoyed within their own school will be extended to other agencies, which is understandably not necessarily the perception of workers in these agencies (Abrams & Gibbs, 2000). Interaction and communication skills are needed to interact with staff from other agencies (Dryfoos, 1995), while stable leadership, both in the schools as in collaborating agencies is seen as key to the maintenance of effective collaboration according to McMahon, Ward, Pruett, Davidson, and Griffith et al. (2000). Cummings et al. (2009) report a wide range of different leadership arrangements in Full-Service Extended Schools, from distributed approaches, were heads would actively involve others in leadership as the perceived complexity of interagency work made it, in their view, impossible to handle on their own, while in others the model was more one of parallel strands, with the head retaining strong overall control while delegating leadership task to a schools-based coordinator. The National College for School Leadership and Demos organised a number of seminars on leadership in extended schools in early 2005. Findings from this seminar suggest that leaders focussed on building capacity across the school and were motivated by a commitment to making a difference in their locality. They also felt a need to allow more freedom for local solutions within the school, which they felt was necessitated by the increased complexity of extended schooling (Craig, 2005).

While, therefore, there is an emerging evidence base concerning multiagency work involving education, the evidence base on the leadership implications for school managers resulting from extended schools is still limited. This would appear to be a key issue, in the sense that both the background of school leaders, as school practitioners and their leadership development will not necessarily have prepared them to take on the challenges of working collaboratively with a range of non-school agencies.

10.2 Methodology

This study aimed to explore interagency work carried out in extended schools from a leadership perspective. In particular, the perceived advantages, disadvantages and barriers to multiagency work in schools were explored, as were the leadership implications, relations to school leadership, and implications for leadership development.

Qualitative case studies were carried out in eight schools in the North-East of England that had been designated Leading Edge schools in this area, and were known for their pioneering of multiagency work. All served socio-economically disadvantaged areas. Most were in small to mid size post-industrial towns and cities, with one being in a former mining village and the other in a large urban conurbation. Of the eight case study schools, five were secondary and three were primary schools. The sample was therefore a purposive one of schools at the leading edge of practice with regard to extended schooling and multiagency work. Therefore, rather than being generalisable, the data from this study can serve as an illustration of the issues that schools that are only starting to embark on multiagency collaboration are likely to face in terms of leadership.

Two-day visits were undertaken to the schools. In each school interviews were undertaken with the head, a member of the Senior Management Team, a Middle Manager, a Classroom Teacher, and a member of staff of a non-education agency with which the school was working (referred to for ease as 'multiagency workers' in the rest of this paper). Documentary evidence, including Ofsted reports, plans, and minutes were collected as well.

Staff from non-school agencies interviewed had a variety of roles, including behaviour support, speech and language therapy and social services, and typically worked across more than one schools.

Interviews were conducted using semi-structured interview schedules. A cross-site analysis of the data was conducted in relation to the overall research questions. The data was analysed using the constant comparative method which involves anticipation, immersion, validation, interpretation, and analysis (Becker, 1958). This four-stage analytical strategy, based on the conventions of sociological fieldwork, has been used in a wide range of studies. In further strengthening claims, particularly in respect to the relationship between practices and outcomes, we took guidance from Schon (1991). Using the ideas of Karl Popper, he argued that the fundamental test for validity is through 'competitive resistance to refutation'. This involves juxtaposing alternate plausible accounts of the phenomenon in question. Schon notes: 'In the absence of an alternate hypothesis, one is likely to be overwhelmed by the obviousness of what one already knows'. Taking account of this challenge, we discussed our interpretations of the data with three colleagues and three practitioners.

10.3 Results

10.3.1 Views on Multiagency Work

Interagency work helps schools avoid isolation and is useful for benchmarking. It extends expertise in the school by growing the knowledge base staff have access to, according to heads:

> *We now have much more expertise, much more experience (middle manager).*

Some respondents felt that interagency work led to the school being more open to the outside, with a greater opportunity for the community to go into the school.

One head felt that interagency involvement made the school 'a nicer place', and allowed staff to broaden their experience, another felt it made his school more 'vibrant'.

The ability to share practice was seen as a major advantage by several interviewees. As one head said

> *The key is, sitting in a multiagency group, someone who has the expertise can tell you, this is just not right.*

A respondent from a primary school described this as a 'mutual learning process', which, however, can only occur where there is trust on both sides. The head of a large secondary school felt that this process allowed him to influence decision making in partner organisations in a way that would not otherwise have been possible. Furthermore, parents feel they get a better and more joined up service.

Schools had often received additional funding to engage in multiagency work, and in three schools this was seen as the main advantage thereof.

Staff directly involved in interagency work tend to be the most positive about it. In the most positive cases, the collaboration with external agencies was described as *enriching and reassuring* (head of department, secondary school). According to a teacher working closely with multiagency staff, *it stops little empires being built, and people are less able to play one of against the other*, while a classroom assistant commented that *It benefited the children, the work with other agencies I've done. I would like to work with more outside agencies.*

Some differences appear in responses depending on the type of agency the respondent worked with. Government agencies, such as social services, tend to be seen as more bureaucratic and difficult to work with than private companies, such as football clubs. One interviewee specifically contrasted his experiences in this way:

> *The work with the local Premiership football club was great, but when we were on the Active City working party with the council there was just talk, but nothing happened.*

On the other hand, the head of one school saw the advantage of multiagency work lying in the ability to get fast targeted support without the bureaucracy that existed before.

Reasons to take on interagency work were varied, and could be distinguished as being more or less instrumental, ranging from *the money was there* (head, secondary school) through *we thought it would enrich the school and extend networks* (head, secondary school), who sees this as a vital part of network development in preparation for a future without LEAs, to statements regarding the need to help all children.

Respondents differed by school in the extent to which they mentioned students. In three schools respondents did not mention benefits to students at all. In the other schools, however, benefits to students were often seen as key. One respondent in a primary school specifically mentioned the ability it fostered to put students and their needs at the heart of the school, while the head of a secondary school mentioned better provision for pupils with significant problems as a key advantage of interagency work. In particular, he had found that they were able to get speedier support thanks to collaboration between schools and social services. This head felt strongly that this allowed the whole child to be addressed and that these services were most effective when locally controlled and school based, provided they were integrated into the daily work of the school, and were *readily available and accessible*, a view shared by respondents in other schools as well. According to the head of a primary school:

> *Children don't just need education, they need caring for overall, so the more people you have feeding in, the more holistic it becomes and the more you can address the whole child, and the more both children and parents benefit.*

The fact that pupils may feel safer and more supported in school was also seen as a major benefit for some pupils.

For multiagency staff interagency work is seen as vital: *I don't see how I could do it without an interagency approach* was one typical comment. The need for collaboration was seen as particularly important in view of the number of professionals that can be involved with one family.

10.3.2 Barriers and Facilitators

The amount of work involved in multiagency work was seen as a key barrier to success by some respondents. According to one head, for example, interagency work takes a lot of effort with little positive feedback if other organisations don't put the same effort in. He commented that with interagency work *we don't always get out of it what we put in*. The time-consuming nature of this type of collaboration was also stressed by a senior manager in another school: *it can be really slow and time hungry, and cuts across teaching time*. Time needs to be made in order to make the collaboration effective *bolt on at the end of the day just doesn't work, everyone is tired and just wants to go home* (head, primary school).

There is also a perceived danger of the effort involved in multiagency work leading to the school's work and capacities to be spread too thinly, and in that way actually being detrimental to the school. Finding the right *balance between the needs of the organisation, your time and the needs of their organisation* was seen as key by one head of department, for example. Lack of time is a common complaint, and one interviewee claimed that multiagency work *can be overwhelming due to the effort it takes* (head, primary school). A lack of distributed leadership may be a contributing factor in some schools, with one head complaining that time was an additional pressure for her due to her staff's inability to take initiative. Not all interviewees saw this as a problem, however. One senior manager commenting that *while time can be an issue, the rewards are so great that it really isn't a problem. I don't see it as a cost.* Slow decision making and compromise were seen as problems by agency staff as well.

An issue that many respondents commented on was the lack of cultural fit between the organisations involved, leading, according to the one head, to a *lack of mutual respect and commitment*, a *clash of priorities* and a clash of cultures leading to problems in properly connecting the different agencies. One head of department described the problem as encountering a *social worker type approach*, which she described as being less concerned with standards and overly concerned with risk. A lack of pace and expectations among social services staff was a common complaint from school staff. Another head of department described agency staff as having *lower standards of professionalism than ourselves*, leading to a conflict of interest as the agency staff were seen as less likely to challenge pupils. According to one interviewee *they (in this case social workers and the police) don't understand the working processes and realities of schools* (deputy head, secondary school). Trust is seen as key here, but is impeded by the cultural differences and different ethos of the organisations involved, the long-term view of many agencies contrasting with the shorter-term performance driven culture of the schools. The extent to which this is mentioned as a problem does differ between schools, with interviewees in one school, for example, stressing respect between partners as a strength of the collaboration: *it works here, because we really value and respect each other* (classroom teacher, primary school). The head of this school felt that *people work together in ways that are compatible with school culture.*

Trying to improve coherence between the different organisations was seen as a key leadership task in interagency work for many interviewees. One complaint was that while when people working on the ground were very enthusiastic when they came together, when they went back to their organisation there could be suspicion of organisations taking each others' resources. Ego clashes were mentioned as a specific problem in one secondary school, where the question of who takes the credit arose, according to the head. The head of another secondary mentioned experiencing some resentment from school staff who see multiagency work as easy:

> *They just come into school from time to time, that is sometimes the impression. They just work with two children, why aren't they making more impact?.*

Agency staff also see cultural differences as a barrier: *we do have very different perspectives sometimes*, and mention the National Curriculum and timetabling as specific constraints to successful interagency working.

> *It's sometimes hard to fit in work with an individual child, because of the curriculum, in the sixth form, where they don't have the national curriculum, I think that makes it easier* (social worker).

They don't always feel fully included in the work of the school, one interviewee describing herself as *although I'm based at the school, I think I'm seen more as a familiar visitor*. This is seen as problematic in terms of their relationship with the school:

> *I think because you are working for another agency, this can be a problem for heads, because they feel they don't have full control over you.*

Shared goals and targets appear to be key if interagency work is to be successful. Targets, goals and their evaluation need to be shared. This factor was mentioned by all interviewees. Both sides need to see benefits *it needs to be a win-win situation* (head of department, secondary school)

In order for interagency work to be successful it needs to be high on the school's list of priorities. Staff at all levels of the organisation need to be involved in the networks and activities. Communication is key: *Name to name communication is essential for it to work* (head of year secondary school) *You've got to get to know people's backgrounds to get to work together* (classroom teacher, primary school). However, communication needs to be based on a real understanding:

> *If you're not careful, the different terminology used by the different agencies will harm communication, the same thing can mean different things, and that is something that needs to be gotten out of the way at the start* (classroom teacher, primary school).

The importance of communication is also stressed by all interviewed agency staff. Building relationships is an important part of this *It's about both, having the formal elements of communication, but also the relationships*. Communication is seen as problematic in some schools, however: *teachers will wonder, why haven't I got information on that kid back yet* (Head of Year, secondary school). However, while open communication is stressed, confidentiality of information is seen as an issue by some interviewees. *Information has to be on a need to know basis, you have to think, sometimes, they really don't need to know that* (middle manager, secondary school).

School structures are generally not seen as problematic for interagency work by either school or agency staff, and there is a clear sense that culture rather than structures determine the success of interagency work. However, where good practice was described shared collaborative planning and easy access to school staff were mentioned.

The success of multiagency work was seen by some interviewees as linked to making clear choices ion what agencies to work with. According one head, interagency work was mainly successful if you worked specifically with those who wanted to work with you, and quickly cut off relationships with those who didn't. This was view was shared by one of the other heads: *Occasionally, you'll get someone who really doesn't want to be here, cos [sic] while in terms of helping children it's great, as far as your career in the health service goes it's not exactly the best thing since sliced bread.* This problem can be exacerbated if meetings are held where people are just invited without having any knowledge or interest in the area: *I have sometimes been asked just to fill a seat* (head, primary school).

In making multiagency work effective, prior experience of school-to-school collaboration was seen as a major help. One of the secondary schools, for example, worked with other schools through its leading edge partnerships, as well as being closely involved in collaboration through the Specialist Schools and Academies Trust. This was seen as providing a good basis for interagency work, though the head commented that it was easier to work with other schools as the benefits were seen to be equal, as was the status of the organisations involved. A history of extensive collaboration with other schools in the area was seen as a useful opportunity to develop these skills in the primary schools involved.

The need for flexibility and regular contact in order to help improve trust and relationships came up in several discussions as key to successful collaboration *You need sensitive approaches, in which sharing occurs firstly in small groups were people have learnt to trust one another* (head of department, secondary school).

Unsurprisingly, additional funding and staff release were generally seen to be desirable in all schools studied.

10.3.3 What Does Success Look Like?

An issue in extended schools is how to judge the success of multiagency collaboration, as multiagency work cannot very easily be judged by the traditional school outcome measures in terms of academic achievement.

The lack of hard targets for much interagency work was seen as problematic by some interviewees, though some solutions, such as surveys of staff on the effectiveness of the work were proposed, and other interviewees, such as the head of one secondary school, argued that in the end interagency work should also lead to higher standards of achievement. The head of a primary school sees *seeing real change* as the measure of success. *Targets mean nothing to me*. Teachers and middle managers interviewed in the school feel that milestones monitored in meetings are the key measure. *Being asked for advice* was mentioned by one interviewee (middle manager, secondary school). In the largest secondary school in the sample efforts were evaluated regularly, and the success of interventions is discussed. Less exclusions were seen as one measure of success, as were changes in pupil attitudes. Having extensive relationships was seen as an indicator of success in itself by one interviewee: *People still want to keep working with you* and *they are still there at the end of the year* (secondary head). The quality of relations established was also seen as important.

While the above views point to a focus on either school-level outcomes or relationships, in some schools the focus was very much more on the individual pupil. In some schools the focus was very much on the personal and social development of pupils. Success is seen as: *Young people's confidence, their ability to manage themselves and their ability to see themselves as valued and valuable* (head, primary school). Similar views were expressed in one of the secondary schools: *If it makes a difference to one pupil it's worthwhile* (head of department).

10.3.4 Leadership

It has recently been argued that collaboration between schools is correlated to more distributed forms of leadership, both enabling these and being enabled by them due to the opportunities for leadership available in these collaborations (West & Muijs, 2006). Therefore, the question can be asked as to whether the same is true for schools collaborating with other agencies.

Leadership styles differed significantly between Heads in the schools studied here, and distributed leadership was not present in all the schools studied. The head of a large secondary school, for example, described his leadership as hands-on, and claimed he could be both autocratic and distributed depending on circumstances and on whether he trusted the individual involved. Overall, though the head indicated that distributed leadership was not the norm in this school *power without responsibility won't work* The head felt that only a minority of staff wanted to take part in leadership, and that heads of department didn't necessarily know how to share leadership, a view confirmed by one head of department who claimed: *I don't know how to delegate or share leadership enough*. An extended leadership team was employed in this school consisting of three deputies and three assistant heads. There is consultation with staff and pupils, though there does not appear to be a great deal of involvement of non-school staff. High standards and high expectations were seen as characteristic of the school by several interviewees.

Similarly, distributed leadership was not common in the smallest of the secondary schools involved, where leadership is largely done by the SMT and the heads of year. The head believed that staff didn't generally want to participate in leadership. *They were offered the opportunity, but most bypassed this* According to him, there were *not enough leaders around*. This view was shared by a member of the SMT, who likewise mentioned the quality of staff as a problem in distributing leadership. Therefore, instead of distributing leadership, an extended SMT was created with 15 members. This situation was improving, however, thanks to the *improved quality of intake from PGCE*, which has meant teachers taking on responsibility at a younger age. The head of this school described his leadership as maverick and unconventional. Several other heads complained of the difficulty of distributing leadership:

> *I kind of assumed that when we discussed something, and a decision was taken, they would go out and implement it, but in practice, for some people, that was wrong* (head, primary school).

This was not necessarily seen as a problem, however. According to the head some staff want to get involved in leadership, but others *come to work, and just do the job and complete their hours. They do a good job, so we need people like that as well.*

In other schools leadership is much more distributed. In another secondary school, which was characterised by a large leadership team, the headteacher was described by staff as 'visionary', while the deputy head exercises the day-to-day management of the school. In this school distributed leadership was encouraged, at least among middle management. As one middle manager commented: *We are fully involved.* Staff were encouraged to take the lead on small projects, and were often singled out for this, in preparation for taking on larger leadership roles. This distribution of leadership was deliberately increased over time. The head had initially lead through strong central control, but had progressively distributed leadership as he felt capacity in the school increase.

A mixed model is represented by an urban secondary school, described by one middle manager as *very much a top-down bottom-up school*, that mixed strong central vision with opportunities for all staff to get involved. A number of teams existed through which the leadership of the school was formalised, including an operational team, a curriculum team, a head of departments team, a heads of year team, and a research and development team alongside the senior management team. These structures were seen as enabling the distribution of leadership within the school. Staff received training and inset to develop their leadership capacities, though not all were involved. As one respondent said: *There is no point to watering the stones, we need to play to the strengths of individuals* (senior manager). The school also had a strong student council. A mixed approach was also seen to be present in one of the primary schools, where the head claimed to use a wide range of leadership styles, and practices consultation widely, while also using wide-ranging executive powers, a view confirmed by other interviewees. A shared view on leadership in the school was not present in all schools studied. In one example, leadership was described as distributive by some interviewees, though others claimed decisions were taken by the SMT alone.

Schools also differ in how interagency was managed. The Senior Management Team was strongly involved in three of the schools. Management of interagency work was largely done by deputy heads in one, while the SMT as a whole was also seen as crucial in the largest secondary school, with elements such as expertise and providing a line of support for other staff being key aspects of their role in supporting multiagency work. Their support was seen as vital if the difficulties of interagency working are to be overcome. The senior leadership team had a less direct role in some of the other schools, in many cases seen as setting out the strategic direction, but not necessarily being that involved with the day-to-day work. The speech therapist working with this school felt that strong leadership and a strong commitment from leadership to interagency working were vital, and distinguished this school from other schools she worked with. *I've worked with schools were leadership was weaker, and that is harder going. Also the same is true in schools were leadership is strong, but there is not really a commitment to interagency work.*

Working with other agencies within an extended school context was seen as requiring some specific additional skills, such as the ability to negotiate, collaborate, and engage with different ways of working. An open-mindedness and ability to take on board different perspectives therefore seemed key, along with the interpersonal skills necessary for this.

> *Leaders need to be less arrogant, more open to the ideas and ways of others* (head, primary school).

> *You've got to realise that agencies work in different ways. I had a tendency to think in the beginning: I could sort you out, make you work more efficiently, but over time I've come to realise, yes, that's fine too* (head, secondary school).

Patience was seen as a second key of the interviewed heads, again pointing to some tension in the work between agencies. Emotional intelligence, awareness of each others' strengths, and weaknesses, and flexibility were mentioned additionally by some interviewees, while one head of this school stressed tact, humility and diplomacy. The head of one of the primary schools felt that a key problem in interagency work was that of leadership style. She claimed that her style was not to everybody's liking, and that in particular the fact that she based her leadership on values while others' based theirs on targets was an issue. *I think those styles get in the way.* Interagency work and collaboration need to be part of the vision of the leadership team, according to the one Head. Stressing the moral purpose of schools, she claimed that education needs to be geared to *the common good, rather than just what's good for our school.*

Time management was seen as another management challenge in interagency working. *You end up spending more ands more time, when you do this, and the question is how to cope with that* (head, secondary school). Leaders also need to make sure that multiagency work is seen as an important part of the school's activities. *It's getting everybody to see its right, really, that could be a problem* (middle manager).

In all schools SMT members and most middle managers have taken part in some form of leadership development, such as NPQH or Leading from the Middle, as well as other courses developed by local Leadership centres. Some agency staff had also had some leadership development, for example through Health Service programmes. This was not universal, however. None had received leadership development specifically tailored for leadership in multiagency contexts.

Most respondents, while feeling that multiagency work requires a specific skill set, did not feel that more formal leadership training was the answer to upskilling them in this area. The exception to this widely held view was one primary Head, who felt that some specialist courses mixed with a portfolio approach and hands-on mentoring would be helpful. Many respondents felt that participation in the National Professional Qualification for Headship (NPGH) had been helpful in preparing them for leading in multiagency contexts, in that some of the learning she experienced there could be transferred to interagency work. One secondary head felt that NPQH had helped him to be less insular and therefore better prepared for multiagency work. Most respondents, however, did not feel that existing training prepared them well for multiagency work. In one school, the introduction of a required management certificate was seen by the head as actually damaging leadership in the school, by focussing mainly on management and *telling people they were doing everything wrong*.

Hands-on mentoring and coaching arrangements were seen as most likely to be useful, and this was reflected in views on leadership development respondents had already participated in. NPQH for example, was rated differentially by respondents, some commenting that it was insufficiently practical with regard to skills such as law and finance needed in school management. Use of role models and shadowing was frequently mentioned.

The head of one urban secondary school felt strongly that leadership development needs a stronger focus on philosophy, values, and moral purpose, as well as needing to look at systems that can foster collaboration better. He sees case studies as potentially most useful to this approach. Some theoretical base is seen as important by many interviewees, as is joint training of staff from the school and different agencies.

10.4 Conclusion

Multiagency work has recently been promoted as key to helping schools address the multiple needs of their pupils, especially in disadvantaged contexts, and there is some evidence from this study that this approach may be fruitful. As was found by Cummings et al. (2009), there is evidence that individual pupils can be helped by multiagency work, but also that some impact on the school as an organisation may occur. A broader perspective, widened expertise, and mutual learning were all mentioned in this regard.

However, it is also clear that multiagency work is complex and challenging, and in many cases has stretched the management capability of schools. A culture clash between agencies and schools is very much in evidence, with the performance-based culture schools in England are compelled to work within not sitting comfortably with what is perceived as both a more bureaucratic and a longer-term approach taken by agency staff. A clear conflict is in evidence between the focus on academic achievement of schools and the focus on affective and social outcomes of agency staff, which evidences itself in complaints about lower standards from some school staff. Clear shared aims and strong and personal communication are essential if the relationship is to be effective, but more attention to what would be successful outcomes is also necessary. The confusion regarding what a successful outcome of multiagency work might be that was evident among interviewees may lead to schools not seeing the value of the work, and falling back on the default position of attention to academic achievement at the expense of other outcomes, thus exacerbating the cultural differences found here. A broader range of outcomes need to be measured officially for this problem to be fully overcome. What is also required is sensitive leadership at the school level, that is prepared to listen and learn, and values different perspectives brought to the table by different actors. Shadowing successful practice and mentoring arrangements are seen as most likely to help develop the additional skills needed to be successful in multiagency work.

An interesting finding from this study concerns the differences between schools in attitudes towards multiagency work. While all were selected on the basis of their strong engagement in multiagency work, it was clear that they differed substantially with regard to approaches, leadership, and the extent to which they saw multiagency work as a boon or a burden to the school. These differences were not related to school phase or size, or indeed to the type of pupils served, but seemed to be linked to two key leadership factors: focus and distribution.

Focus refers to the perceived purposes of multiagency work. As mentioned above these differed strongly, and varied from very instrumental goals focussed on material benefits to the school, to goals based around moral purpose with regard to helping the whole child. Distribution refers to the extent to which leadership in the school was distributed or largely the preserve of the Senior Management Team. It would appear from this, admittedly limited, sample that where both strong moral purpose around multiagency work and distributed leadership occurred, perceptions of multiagency work were more positive. The former is not surprising, in that, in view of the heavy demands of managing multiagency schools, the additional motivation provided by moral purpose around the activity would be essential to putting in place the additional effort involved for example in putting in place strong communication around the value of multiagency work, understanding different ways of working and dealing with the bureaucratic requirements involved. The second factor, distributed leadership, may be important for similar reasons. It is probably not possible for senior managers to take on the many additional tasks that may result from multiagency work without distributing leadership. Getting agency and school staff to take on leadership in their own collaborations may lead to greater understanding across the school, and practically help individual pupils. Furthermore, the finding that staff most closely involved with multiagency work are most enthused by it suggests that by involving them in leadership it is more likely that their enthusiasm is translated to other school staff, and indeed to the Senior Management Team.

Finally, it is clear that while multiagency work can be beneficial in serving at-risk pupils, it is by no means a panacea (or any more so than other initiatives), and that to be successful it does require a lot of work to acculturate both agency staff and schools. If extended schools are to become an effective part, of, or even the mainstay of, our education system, policy makers and practitioners will have to reform systems and accountability mechanisms to ensure greater congruence in values and goals. Multiple and conflicting targets couples with limited accountability mechanisms certainly do not make this easier.

Part III
Successful Collaboration

Chapter 11
Reflections on Networking and Collaboration

11.1 Challenges and Possibilities

The UK government, along with other Western governments, has argued that the raising of standards must also promote equity: that the emphasis on raising attainment must not simply benefit children who are already performing at a high level. Implemented properly, and supported by the various inclusion initiatives, the standards agenda is, it is argued, of even greater potential benefit to previously low-attaining children in poorly performing schools: it is about excellence for the many, not just the few.

Yet the national strategies to raise standards and other accountability measures such as the 'No Child Left Behind' legislation in the US, whatever their benefits, have tended to reduce the flexibility with which schools can respond to the diverse characteristics of their students. Our research demonstrates that this is a particular problem for schools that are formally categorised as performing poorly, since the short-term pressure to deliver satisfactory 'metrics' that this demands, can postpone the development of strategies necessary for longer-term improvement. And, as is evident from studies of schools that had made sustained progress, despite the drag-anchor of being identified as 'below floor targets' (West, Ainscow, & Stanford, 2005), head teachers are acutely aware of such pressures.

Whilst the need to escape such designations can be useful in galvanising early efforts, since the designation itself becomes a common enemy upon which energies can be focussed, it may also limit and inhibit ambition—amongst students and teachers alike.

Nevertheless, our analysis of the experiences also offers some reasons for optimism, not least in that it suggests that the system has considerable untapped potential to improve itself. There are, we have noted, skills, knowledge and, most importantly, creativity within schools, and within their local communities, that can be mobilised to improve educational provision. We have seen, for example, how school staff groups can come together to strengthen and increase the impact of one another's efforts; we have seen the impact when head teachers pool their knowledge and experience for the benefit of a particular school, or for a group of schools; we have seen the potential for cooperation between schools and their local authority,

D. Muijs et al., *Collaboration and Networking in Education*,
DOI 10.1007/978-94-007-0283-7_11, © Springer Science+Business Media B.V. 2011

and with the wider community; and, running through all our work, we have seen the potential of partnerships between school staff and researchers.

All of this demonstrates what can be achieved when those who have a stake in urban education engage in authentic collaborative activity. Of course, collaboration has itself been a regular feature of national policy in recent years, best illustrated by Excellence in Cities and the Leadership Incentive Grant, both initiatives specifically targeted on schools in challenging urban environments. Nevertheless, and despite this press for greater collaboration within and between schools, there has been a tendency to view urban schools through a deficit lens, focussing on what they lack rather than the resources that they can draw on. As a result, it has often been assumed that externally driven strategies are the only feasible means of achieving improvement. Whilst recent work leaves us in no doubt about the importance of additional resources as a stimulus to school to school collaboration (Ainscow et al., 2006), we are also aware of the potency of local ownership and local ideas. Indeed, our experiences suggest that national improvement strategies have, too often, fallen into the trap of overlooking the evidence that local interpretation and adaptation can shape and strengthen the way proposals are implemented. It seems to us that this helps to explain why these initiatives have had rather mixed effects.

Of course, the pressures arising from inspection and from the publishing of inspection reports and test and examination results have certainly focussed minds. In some instances, this has also inspired a degree of rethinking and experimentation. However, it has sometimes encouraged staff to take a rather insular approach—after all, what one school 'contributes' to the success of another does not appear in any league table. At the same time, the political imperative to achieve rapid results, particularly the desire to identify strategies that 'work' and then to 'up-scale' these through centrally determined prescriptions, has created barriers to progress. Further, the tendency to designate some schools as failing, or causing concern, can place restrictions on the willingness of those involved to take risks.

However, we remain optimistic that schools can find ways to work together and with their communities that will enable some of the disadvantages of location and catchment to be overcome. The remainder of this paper develops this argument, giving examples of collaboration between schools, and the impact of such collaboration. It sets out our understanding of what collaboration means, and our speculations about the factors that encourage schools to enter into sustained collaborative arrangements with one another. Finally, it concludes with what we feel is needed if collaboration is to become an important ingredient in the school improvement process.

Our findings reported here are based on a detailed analysis of case studies of collaborative practice in urban authorities in different parts of the country. Both process and outcome data were analysed and compared in identifying the sample, which represents instances where collaboration seems to have had significant, positive impact on student experiences and outcomes, as measured by current metrics for school performance and as judged by Ofsted inspection teams. As far as possible, findings and interpretations were validated with appropriate stakeholder groups.

11.2 Impact of Collaboration

Of course, the impact of collaboration has varied considerably from place to place. While in some instances, it has led to interesting explorations of the possibilities of schools working together, many of these initiatives remain fragile. Indeed, there are instances where the resources provided to underpin collaborative working have simply been hived off to serve the purposes of individual schools. There are, however, some contexts in which school-to-school collaboration seems to have had a significant impact on both practice and on learning outcomes. These examples confirm that such arrangements do have an enormous potential for fostering system-wide improvement, particularly in urban contexts. More specifically, they begin to show how collaboration between schools can provide an effective means of solving immediate problems, such as staff shortages; how they can have a positive impact in periods of crisis, such as during the closure of a school; and, how, in the longer run, schools working together can contribute to the raising of aspirations and attainment in schools that have had a record of low achievement. There is also evidence that collaboration can help to reduce the polarisation within the education system, to the particular benefit of those students who are on the edges of the system and performing relatively poorly. The approaches to collaboration we have documented in this book vary considerably in style, and in terms of their impact on practice and learning outcomes. The impact may be direct or indirect, short term or longer term. We enlarge on this below.

11.3 Direct Impact Activities

We note that activities that have a direct and immediate impact on achievement tend to be *relatively* easy to implement, as we illustrate in the following brief examples from the work of various collaboratives:

- One collaborative has prepared a detailed analysis of the strengths and weaknesses of all the subject departments in all schools. This means that interventions can draw on the best practice available to focus on areas of need. So, for example, in one school there is a problem in the Science department, and an Advanced Skills Science Teacher from another school in the group is seconded to the school 1 day each week to support development.
- Several of the schools in another collaborative were experiencing difficulties with English teaching. Since they all had rather inexperienced heads of department, the collaborative decided to appoint an experienced teacher to act as consultant. The contributions of the consultant varied from school to school, depending on need and circumstances. In some cases she supported heads of department in developing their leadership practices, in others she worked with teaching staff in developing schemes of work and resources and on some occasions, she coached teachers with regard to their classroom practices.
- Some schools, particularly those that have a relatively poor reputation, have found it difficult to attract suitably qualified teachers for some areas of the

curriculum. On the other hand, schools that are seen as being more successful tend to face far fewer difficulties, even within the same geographical area. The worry is that these inequities act in ways that further widen the quality of experience between high-achieving and low-achieving schools. Music, not a mainstream subject, but one that many students enjoy, offers a good example of this phenomenon. At one point, three schools in a network of schools were unable to offer music lessons at all, simply because they could attract no qualified staff. At the same time, students in another school in the locality had access during a typical week to 14 music teachers, both school-based and peripatetic. The collaborative identified music as an area for joint development, and set up a system that spread the teaching of music specialists between schools. As well as providing additional funding to attract new staff and encourage much wider participation in music across the schools, the network was able to offer teaching jobs that involved work in a number of schools, making them much more attractive to potential recruits.

11.4 Strengthening Capacity

Some strategies involve processes that are intended to increase the capacity of schools and of their staffs to offer a stronger curriculum and more effective teaching arrangements. This notion of capacity-building (Hopkins et al., 1994) is an important one, if schools could simply increase their impact on students by changing policies, it might be expected that they would have already done so. Unfortunately, when schools have not done so, it is usually because the school community does not have the capacity to implement changes necessary to underpin improvements.

By their nature, such changes take longer to implement, as illustrated in the following examples:

- Two capacity-building activities are gradually deepening the collaboration between the eight schools in one network, whilst addressing specific areas of work that require further development. First of all, a series of 'self-help groups' have been created that bring together key staff who are responsible for similar tasks in their schools. Each of these groups is coordinated by an individual from a different school in the network. Current areas of focus for such groups include: curriculum development, timetable planning, inclusion, pastoral care, and post-16 arrangements. Plans are being developed so that all the schools will coordinate the post-16 timetable. This will mean that staff and students can move between schools in order to maximise choices and strengthen pedagogy across the collaborative.
- One collaborative has developed a staff development strategy that involves representatives from each of the schools, working together to strengthen particular areas of practice. So, for example, heads of department took part in a 2-day workshop provided by a team from another Local Education Authority (LEA), and

there are follow-up arrangements to support them in implementing action plans with their own staff teams. The agenda for the workshop, including the use of evidence and the monitoring of teaching and learning, was customised to address needs that had been determined by key insiders within the various schools. One recently appointed departmental head explained that it had focussed on exactly the issues facing her department. She particularly valued the opportunity to learn alongside more experienced colleagues from other schools in the group.

- Gradually, the idea of sharing teaching resources in one network has developed in a way that seems to be valuable in relation to the appointment and retention of staff. Indeed, one of the heads argues that for collaboration to work, 'shared staffing is essential'. So far, a range of approaches have been explored. For example, a joint advertisement was very successful in attracting teachers to the collaborative who may not have applied to those individual schools with relatively poor levels of performance. Meanwhile, the need to appoint part-time posts has on some occasions been avoided, by combining posts across schools posts. A joint staffing plan was put in place, which covers joint training arrangements for post holders, such as those who take on the role of second-in-department. Finally, trainee teachers move between the partner schools during their placements, and there is an intention to become a joint training school.
- Shared inset events within the network provide opportunities to meet teachers from other schools. These are valued by many teachers. As one teacher commented, *This was better than school INSET, because it's good to get out of the comfort zone, the limited way of seeing things in your own school.* Younger teachers, in particular, echoed this sentiment, noting that they had never experienced events where staff were so explicitly (and in many cases literally) putting things on the table for others to borrow and make use of.

11.5 Responding to Crises

In some instances, individual schools have faced crisis points. Collective responses have been seen as valuable in helping to resolve very difficult situations arising within a single school. For example:

- A striking example of the value of one network was seen in its contribution to one of the member schools, which had been placed in 'special measures' following inspection. One of the most straightforward aspects of this was financial, in that the school was not required to contribute into the collective 'kitty', thus making available additional resources to tackle immediate priorities. When it came down to direct practical assistance, it was noticeable that the issues to do with teaching and learning that were at the centre of the 'special measures' agenda, were adopted as development priorities across all of the schools. This meant that teachers from across the schools were to work alongside colleagues in the struggling school, helping it to improve practice and to emerge from its temporary period of crisis.

- The final cohort of students left at a school that is closing tend to suffer, as key staff seek other posts, leaving increasingly negative atmosphere amongst those students and staff who are left behind. One collaborative made a major contribution in helping one school to avoid such a situation. They did this by working together on joint projects, sharing resources, and requiring staff newly appointed to other schools in the collaborative to work in the school during the first year of their contracts, bringing a renewed sense of life and vigour. In the summer of 2004, 150 Year 11 students in a school about to close down attained what were the best GCSE results at the school for years.

11.6 Sustaining Improvements

The examples we have presented so far illustrate activities whose impacts tend to be relatively rapid, but are often temporary in nature. However, we also have evidence suggesting that certain types of developments are proving to be promising in relation to more sustainable improvements. Inevitably, these activities are more complex and involve processes which take longer to evolve, not least because they most often require the negotiation of common priorities and shared values. They also require an investment of human resources, in order to create a framework for management and coordination, as we see in the following examples:

- In one network, the school that has Leading Edge status tends to take the lead in the majority of the improvement efforts. One of the deputies from that school acts as overall improvement coordinator, and is seconded from her duties for 2 days a week to fulfil this role. The head of that particular school talked with pride about what had been achieved so far across the network, whilst also commenting on the impact of these efforts on staff within her own school. So, for example, she explained about the impact on one of her ASTs of supporting developments elsewhere: *She has gained personally and professionally. In fact, it has been fantastic training for her. It has given her a new perspective.* The head went on to say that this teacher was likely to be promoted to a post of head of department in the near future as a result of the developments in her thinking and practice.
- The group of three schools which currently make up one network are increasingly working towards becoming a single federation, sharing responsibility for progress in all of the partner schools and pooling resources for teaching, for building maintenance, and various educational projects. The close working relationships have emerged from the recognition of the mutual benefits of sharing. All schools feel that they have gained from the collaborative working arrangements that have been set up, and are seeking ways to secure these arrangements in the longer term through changes in governance.
- Another network now has in post a consultant head teacher, jointly funded, who works 2 days each week to support developments across the member schools. It is clearly a great advantage that this person is a highly regarded, practising head

from a nearby LEA. A number of other 'outsiders', including two officers from the LEA and a consultant from the Leadership development Unit at the University of Manchester, add further resources to the developments that are taking place. Perhaps the key to this is that all of these contributions are seen as being part of a single improvement strategy.

11.7 Sharing in Leadership

In terms of moving the idea of school-to-school collaboration forward, the issue of shared leadership is, we believe, a central driver. This requires leadership practices that involve many stakeholders in sharing responsibility for improving the outcomes for all learners in all of the schools within a collaborative. Often this necessitates significant changes in beliefs and attitudes, and new relationships, as well as improvements in practice. For example:

- Responsibility for the management of one network is shared by the eight head teachers, who meet each month. There is also a programme of 'learning walks', where heads visit each other to help in reviewing existing practices. It is anticipated that as relationships deepen and trust grows, these peer review visits will take on a more challenging style. An interesting test of the depth of commitment that already exists occurred as a result of a recent fire that destroyed part of the building in one of the schools. Immediately, other schools offered help, including accommodation and replacement schemes of work. One teacher commented: 12 *months ago that would not have happened.*

11.8 Roles and Responsibilities

It seems, therefore, that the perspective and skills of head teachers are central to an understanding of what needs to happen in order that the potential power of collaboration can be mobilised. Their visions for their schools, their beliefs about how they can foster the learning of all of their students, and their commitment to the power of inter-dependent learning, appear to be key influences. All of this means, of course, that replication of these processes in other schools will be difficult, particularly if those in charge are unwilling or unable to make fundamental changes in working patterns. This being the case, there is a very strong case for providing head teachers with professional development opportunities that will support them in taking this work forward.

The emphasis on school level leadership has very significant implications for the roles of LEA staff, too. It means that they have to adjust their priorities and ways of working in response to collaborative arrangements that are led from within schools. Sometimes this leads to misunderstandings and tensions. For example:

- The development of one network as a relatively autonomous structure raised interesting questions about the role of LEA staff. The head teachers were clearly enthusiastic about the practice of collaboration as it had developed during the first year. However, they were also increasingly aware of the need to define their own agenda. Up until September 2003, it was evident that LEA officers took responsibility for setting the agenda, and for running the collaborative's meetings. As the group became a more solid structure, LEA staff began to consider which other developments and initiatives should be linked to it, and at one point they issued an agenda for a meeting that outlined these. This seemed to raise alarm bells with some head teachers, and phone calls amongst them proliferated as they checked on one another's reactions. The next day, they informed the LEA representative that it would be the collaborative that would draw up the meeting agenda, that the meeting would be chaired by one of the head teachers, and that the LEA representative would be seen as a participant and a partner. In making this stand, the head teachers felt themselves to be exercising a powerful choice about their own future. At the same time, some LEA colleagues recognised this development as being in line with the strengthening and maturing of the collaborative.

There is then, ample evidence within these cases that collaboration between schools has contributed significantly to the ways these schools go about their business. And, remembering that these examples were chosen because they featured groups of schools where student performance has improved more rapidly than is general for schools in difficult urban contexts, it requires no great leap of imagination to posit that collaboration has accordingly contributed to the improvement in student outcomes. But there is no simple equation linking these. Indeed, it is a complex relationship, that involves a range of factors, and the commitment to raise expectations, of teachers and students alike, and the capacity to engage with and manage change are important components.

11.9 Raising Expectations

There is evidence that when schools seek to develop more collaborative ways of working, this can have an impact on how teachers perceive themselves and their work. Specifically, comparisons of practice can lead teachers to view underachieving students in a new light. Rather than simply presenting problems that are assumed to be insurmountable, such students may be perceived as providing feedback on existing classroom arrangements. In this way they may be seen as sources of understanding as to how these arrangements might be developed in ways that could be of benefit to all members of the class.

However, research suggests that developments in practice, particularly amongst more experienced teachers, are unlikely to occur without some exposure to what teaching actually looks like when it is being done differently, and exposure to someone who can help teachers understand the difference between what they are doing and what they aspire to do. It also seems that this sort of problem has to be solved at the individual level before it can be solved at the organisational level. Indeed, there is evidence that increasing collaboration can sometimes result in teachers coming together to reinforce existing practices rather than confronting the difficulties they face in different ways. This is why leadership is such a key factor in ensuring that collaboration involves both support and challenge.

11.10 Managing Change

By and large the evidence is that schools find it difficult to cope with change, particularly where this involves modifications in thinking and practice. In recent years English schools have had to respond to a multitude of new policies aimed at raising standards. A close scrutiny of what has happened where collaboration has led to school improvement suggests that this has been given additional impetus by external pressure. And, like other social organisations undergoing significant transformation, in schools that are under pressure to change the search is on for what Michael Fullan describes as 'order and correctness'. Teachers seeking 'correctness' will often experience ambiguity and confusion in times of change. Equally, it is difficult to establish order when faced with ambiguous situations.

It seems, then, that those who can help to create a sense of common purpose in such contexts can bring about change. This may, in part at least, throw some light on what has occurred in the contexts we have described. Unusual and challenging factors, emanating as they do from both outside and inside schools, have created a sense of ambiguity. Changing demands, again from both outside and inside the school precipitate disorder. The collaborative arrangements introduced by some groups of head teachers have helped to resolve these problems, and, in so doing, they are also drawing different school staffs together behind broadly similar principles.

Research suggests that ambiguity in organisations increases the extent to which action is guided by values and ideology. Consequently, the values of 'powerful people' (i.e. those who can reduce ambiguity) affect what the organisation is and what it can become. Thus, those who resolve ambiguity for themselves and others can implant a new set of values in an organisation, which creates a new set of relevancies and competencies, and, in so doing, introduces a source of innovation. In this way ambiguity sets the scene for organisations to learn about themselves and their environments, allowing them to emerge from their struggles with uncertainty as reinvigorated and more purposeful communities.

11.11 Understanding What Helps Collaboration to Develop

Our own understanding of the potential of collaborative working practices has been influenced by the ideas of Wenger (1998), Senge (1990), and Hargreaves, D., (2003b). Wenger, in putting forward his notion of 'communities of practice', describes the transfer and creation of knowledge within the workplace. Essentially, the members of a work community pass on their knowledge and ideas to one another through processes of 'negotiation' in which common meanings are established.

'New' knowledge acquired in this way can then be tested out in practice—though inevitably it will be modified as it is subjected to new experiences and contexts. In this way, as ideas are moved around within the community, passing from practitioner to practitioner, they are continually modified and refined. In this way, it becomes possible for knowledge to be re-cycled around the community and returned to the originator—though transformed through the process. Thus, the virtuous circle is completed, with knowledge and understanding increased through each iteration.

Senge, in his writings on learning organisations, suggests that knowledge within organisations takes two forms—the explicit and the tacit. Explicit knowledge (which will embrace established wisdom), is relatively easy to transfer, but is likely to be generalised rather than specific. On the other hand, tacit knowledge is caught rather than deliberately passed on, but can only be caught if the right circumstances exist. Consequently, what can be achieved through explicit and tacit exchanges is limited—learning organisations need to find ways to generate tacit-to-explicit and explicit-to-tacit transfers. Again, our conception of collaborative practice is that it provides just such an opportunity, as individuals work together on common goals, sharing and using one another's knowledge and, through the processes of sharing, reflection and re-cycling, creating new knowledge.

David Hargreaves (2003b) also notes the tacit nature of much of teachers' knowledge, when explaining why it has proved so difficult to transfer good practice from one teacher to another. This leads him to conclude that what he describes as 'social capital' is needed within the teaching communities. Social capital here represents shared values and assumptions that, because they are commonly 'owned' by community members, are available for all members of the community to draw on when transferring knowledge and understandings. For him, building social capital involves the development of networks based on mutual trust, within which good practice can spread in natural ways.

Bearing these ideas in mind, we suggest that collaboration within and between schools is a practice that can both transfer existing knowledge and, more importantly, generate context specific 'new' knowledge. Further, our own research gives strong indications of how such processes can be initiated and managed. At the same time, these experiences also point to certain conditions that are necessary in order to make collaboration effective, which we will discuss further in the following two chapters

11.12 From Collaboration to Collegiality

The research summarised in this paper has led us to formulate a typology of the sorts of relationships that can exist within a network of schools. This points to the need for moves towards deeper, more sustainable arrangements, and suggests the steps involved, as follows:

Association – This is the traditional pattern, where there are some links between schools through occasional LEA meetings and in-service events. By and large, however, this does not involve sharing of knowledge or resources.

Cooperation – This is where closer links develop through participation in meetings and activities that provide opportunities to contribute experiences. As a result there may be some incidental sharing of knowledge and resources.

Collaboration – This involves schools in working together to address particular problems or challenges. By its nature such activities requires the sharing of knowledge and resources.

Collegiality – This involves a longer-term relationship between schools that includes the sharing of responsibility in an inter-dependent way. It leads to the bringing together of knowledge and resources within an agreed set of values.

Bearing this typology in mind, the aim must be to foster moves towards more powerful inter-dependent relationships that can strengthen the capacity of all schools to deliver *a decent all-round education for all pupils.* In this regard, the distinction made by Fielding (1999) between 'collaboration' and 'collegiality' is particularly helpful. He characterises 'collaboration' as being driven by a set of common concerns, narrowly functional, and focussed strongly on intended gains. In such contexts, the partners in a collaborative activity are regarded as a resource, or a source of information. Fielding goes on to suggest that collaboration is, therefore, a plural form of individualism in which participants are typically intolerant of time spent on anything other than the task in hand. He argues that once the driving force behind collaboration is weakened, the task has been completed or priorities have changed, such collaborative working arrangements may dissipate, disappear, or become more tenuous. 'Collegiality', on the other hand, is characterised as being much more robust. It is rooted in shared ideals and aspirations, and pursues mutually valued social ends. Collegiality is, therefore, by definition, less reliant upon narrowly defined and predictable 'gains'.

We have found that, in practice, instances of schools working together usually do not fall neatly into either collaborative or collegial activity. Indeed, it may be that collaboration has to be a forerunner to collegiality. In other words, stakeholders may experience the practical benefits of collaborating when the outcomes are clearly defined, whilst seeking to develop a common language and shared aspirations that might, in the longer term, provide a basis for collegiality.

Amongst secondary schools themselves more now needs to be done to strengthen the strategy of collaboration such that it takes on a greater sense of collegiality. Our view is that this will be achieved by encouraging head teachers to take on collective responsibility for the operation. More specifically, the aim must be to develop more collegial relationships, based on a common commitment to improvement across schools, and to principles of equity and social justice. Provided heads genuinely feel that they are in control of the agenda that are so defined, we would be optimistic that this could be achieved. In our discussions with heads, we found none that did not believe in the idea of collaborating with other schools.

11.13 Conclusion

As we have explained, the successful use of collaboration is far from straightforward within the English context, where competition and choice continue to be the major driving forces of national education policy. This is why powerful levers are needed that will challenge existing assumptions and, at the same time, move thinking and practice forward. There appears to be a growing body of evidence, from the United States as well as the UK, indicating that collaboration between schools can deliver a number of benefits for students, for teachers, for schools. Our own research points to certain conditions that are necessary in order to make such school-to-school collaborations effective. In summary, these involved appropriate incentives, shared responsibility for success, leaders who understand how to collaborate, common priorities for improvement, informed external support, and an overriding belief that schools working together for the benefit of all of their students is preferable to competing in order to benefit the few in any particular school.

In our view, the absence of such conditions will mean that attempts to encourage schools to work together are likely to result to time-consuming talk, which sooner or later will be dropped. These conclusions are in themselves important for subsequent national initiatives that invest resources in the idea of schools working in partnership.

Chapter 12
Successful Networking: In-School Conditions

In order for networks to be successful, a number of internal conditions need to be present. In this chapter we will discuss some of these key factors, and how they can be achieved.

12.1 Clear Goals and Mission

A first factor that will determine not just the success, but in all likelihood the sustainability of a network is the existence of a set of shared goals and a shared mission (West & Muijs, 2006). The question of what the network is for should be starting point for the formation and development of the network. Unfortunately, there are all too many examples in education of networks that have developed not because of a clear goal but for other reasons, such as the availability of financial resources that are dependent on networking, coercion from local or national authorities or geographical location.

Where this is the case, collaboration frequently either never comes properly off the ground, meaning that potential benefits are never accrued, or else collapses, often in recrimination and misunderstanding. A further issue is that if no clear goals and mission have been agreed upon at the start it will not be possible to develop an optimal network configuration or structure.

For all these reasons, network actors, under the auspices of the network designer, need to start the process by developing agreement and joint understanding of goals. This is more than just putting together a mission statement or contract. Cultural differences can mean that goals or even terms are understood differently in different schools, an issue that becomes even more acute in collaborations with other agencies, storing up trouble for the future. A series of meetings in which the goals are thrashed out and clarified fully, so a shared understanding develops, is therefore a key activity when setting up the network.

In kind, effective network goals are not that different from effective goals for individual organisations. Like the goals of individual organisations, network goals need to be limited in number, with no more than four or five goals being present. Too many goals leads to a lack of focus and the likelihood than none will be achieved. This problem is exacerbated in networks as a multitude of goals leads to a likelihood

D. Muijs et al., *Collaboration and Networking in Education*,

DOI 10.1007/978-94-007-0283-7_12,

that different organisations will focus on different goals, and/or attach different levels of importance to them, leading once again to misunderstanding and a lack of action coordination.

Goals need to be clearly formulated, and linked to clear actions. They also, crucially in networks, need to be clearly more achievable in a network context than by individual actors. They need to have clear benefits to all organisations within the networks, or lead to an overarching outcome that is of importance and relevance to all network actors. Goals also need to be measurable, so they can be clearly monitored for achievement. It must be clear what contribution individual organisations can and should make to achieving the goal.

Discussing goals and mission requires an openness on the part of participants, and a willingness to innovate and go beyond the traditional ways the organisation works.

An important element of this creation of shared goals is the development of a sense of collective responsibility for bringing about improvements in all the partner organisations. This is often a major cultural change in schools working in a competitive environment, and is linked not just to having shared goals, but to what these goals are. In particular, a foregrounding of social justice and a concern for all pupils in the area rather than just my school are important values in successful networks.

12.2 Finding the Right Partner Schools

A key factor to making networking successful is finding an appropriate partner school or organisation to work with. In many cases schools are chosen on geographical grounds, such as when local area networks or partnerships are formed. There are some good reasons for doing this, not least the fact that the coordination of local school provision can help provide a more coordinated approach which can reduce issues like one school's exclusions becoming another school's problem. However, local area collaboration is not by any means the only possible approach, and it can be problematic where competition between schools is strong, engendering an element of mistrust and sometimes a lack of willingness to share data and best practice with competitors. Also, locality is not the sole determinant of organisational culture, so misunderstandings may emerge due to cultural differences even between schools serving neighbouring or overlapping catchment areas. As we saw in the chapter on multiagency collaboration, a lot of these problems can become even more acute when working with non-school organisations. Key therefore is to try and work with organisations that share cultural understandings and values, and this is something that needs to be carefully explored during the set-up phase. A finding from some studies (e.g. Muijs, Ainscow, & West, 2007) is that collaborations can work particularly well and be particularly easy to set up when the schools involved share a common denomination, such as where two Catholic schools work together. This is most likely to be the result of the values and beliefs shared by these schools. This need for similarities and a shared world view is supported by constructivist organisational theory and Durkheimian theory, which both suggest that a fit of cultures and common understandings are essential to effective collaboration.

As suggested by social capital theory, another essential aspect is to work with organisations that provide complementarity in terms of what they have to offer. Schools that are strong in different curriculum areas, or that offer different vocational specialisms can complement each other well and can make good partners. With non-school organisations such as social services the complementarities are often easier to find, but the cultural gap may be larger, a fact that means that it is often a good idea to spend significant time on working with the partner organisations before the start of collaboration to try and work through any misunderstandings and create understanding and congruence.

12.3 Establishing Clear Communication Channels

In view of the difficulties involved in collaboration and networking, and the room for misunderstanding, communication between all the partners is absolutely crucial. Communication flows are hard enough to effectively organise within an organisation, let alone within a collaborative, and this is therefore a key task.

Firstly, the reasons for communication need to be made clear from the outset. Where the initiative has been taken by senior management, staff lower down the school hierarchy may be unclear on what the potential benefits of the collaboration may be, and in many cases have even been found not to be aware that their school was part of a network (Muijs et al., 2007). Therefore, in much the same way that one would need to communicate the benefits and working of any type of change programme extensively and repeatedly (Kotter, 1998), the same is true of a new networking or collaborative activity. Initial set-up meetings and events with staff from all participating schools can raise awareness, help people to get to know one another and set out the aims and goals of the collaboration.

A key role in effective communication is played by electronic network and communication systems. Wherever possible network partners should try to integrate their electronic communication systems and databases. The merging of databases can be a particularly powerful way of looking at between-school as well as within-school variation, and for the logging and follow up of good practice.

However, electronic communication is obviously not the be all and end all of effective communication. There is a clear need for the setting up of sufficient opportunities for face-to-face interaction, and this especially for those members of staff who you want to benefit from the collaboration. One of the best ways to encourage the benefits of collaboration to spread across the participating schools or organisations is by setting up working groups of teachers and middle managers to take action around specific issues, for example improving provision in a particular curriculum area, developing best practice in a particular pedagogy like group work, or developing a practice like assessment for learning. Such working groups can help blend teams from different school and create genuine networking. Creating multiple points of contact is key here, and this is often best done with some overarching management of the network (see Chapter 13).

Communication becomes an even more important issue in interagency collaboration, with its concomitant cultural and procedural differences. Openness and visibility of procedures by all organisations in the network is one of the main issues that needs addressing to make this kind of collaboration work. Therefore, networks need to put in place systems for sharing information, and wherever possible, try to develop interoperability of IT and other systems so that necessary information is accessible to all partners (Goldsmith & Eggers, 2004). Obviously, when working with young people privacy and data protection issues do limit openness to some extent, but much information can be usefully shared if systems allow it. One of the difficulties of information sharing is that quite a lot of important information in organisations is tacit rather than explicit. How to share this information is a key management challenge, and requires the setting up of spaces for regular communication, where participants in the different schools or organisations in the network can come together to share and to create new shared realities and knowledge. This again points not only to the importance of face-to-face meetings, but also to the usefulness of setting up virtual spaces, such as online Virtual Learning Environments, for information sharing and creation.

12.4 Creating Trust

Another key issue in networking is trust. Trust between schools is usually based on shared values and personal relations between staff active in the network. While trust at the outset is desirable, where that is not the case trust may emerge over the course of collaborating through interaction between the partners. A step-by-step approach to building trust through small-scale collaborations before going on to deeper relationships has been found to be effective in this regard, with partners being open about mistakes made in that process (Bryk & Raudenbusch, 2002).

Creating trust can be hard, especially where schools have previously been competitors, or had very different organisational cultures. In some local authorities, the issue of competition leading to mistrust has been dealt with by getting schools to form networks that do not serve the same catchment area and that therefore don't compete for the same pupils. Similarly, chains of Academies have formed of schools in different locations, who again don't compete directly for students. The argument against this type of arrangement is that while it works well in limiting competition within the network, it doesn't lead to a coordinated local approach and leaves the competitive situation locally unchanged.

However, when these options are not available, specific measures need to be taken to build up trust.

Cognitive convergence is a key element in building trust, and sustained contact can help achieve or broaden this, especially if there are tangible successes emerging from the collaboration at a fairly early stage. It is a well-known finding that interaction can produce homogeneity of beliefs as well as being more likely if homogeneity is pre-existing (Muijs, 1997). Cognitive convergence becomes particularly important where inevitable disagreements arise. Where cognitive convergence exists it becomes easier to discuss these and work them out without misconceptions arising (McAllister, 1995).

However, as well as trust, a number of studies in education have recently found a clear contractual arrangement to be conducive to the effectiveness of networks (Chapman & Allen, 2005; Lindsay et al., 2005), a finding backed up by research in the business sector (Nooteboom, 1996). This may point in part to a lack of trust underlying the networks in these cases, which may be the result of the somewhat coercive nature of many of these networks where external agencies such as the Specialist Schools Trust and Local Authorities have put considerable pressure on 'weak' and 'strong' school to work together. However, the evidence does suggest that some form of contractual agreement is helpful in terms of avoiding misunderstandings and resentment later on. Such contracts should not be overly detailed though, not least as lengthy haggling over detailed points has been found to be non-conducive to the building of a trusting relationship. Part of developing trust is developing a sense of collective responsibility and ownership of outcomes (Ainscow & West, 2005). Where trust is combined with mutual dependence, collaborative relationships tend to be at their deepest and most long-lasting (Nooteboom, 2004). Trust is also related to embeddedness, which is seen as key to allowing social exchanges to go more smoothly (Borgatti & Foster, 2003).

Findings suggest that where relations between schools are unequal (see above) it is necessary to at least acknowledge the strengths of all partners (Chapman & Allen, 2005; Lindsay et al., 2005). A perception of equality can be enhanced through relatively simple measures, such as holding meetings outside of the school building on neutral ground, as a way of limiting the power differential. Where unequal partnerships are to work, there is some (albeit limited) evidence that it is necessary for the better school to confront the partner over problems and change a small number of staff quickly if necessary. A small support team should be sent to the partner school to provide the necessary support (Lindsay et al., 2005).

12.5 Capacity for Improvement

If schools are to collaborate effectively, it will help if they already have capacity to collaborate and improve. This will be facilitated where collaboration and openness already exist in the school. Forms of distributed leadership in school have been found to be related to more effective collaboration between schools, largely due to the greater capacity for leadership in the school, which allows more people to take on roles leading collaborative activities in the network. Interestingly, there is convergent evidence that collaboration itself may enhance leadership capacity and distributed leadership in schools, not least because of the opportunities for leadership afforded by work in the network (see Chapter 14).

Harris (2001) defines capacity building as being concerned with creating the conditions, opportunities and experiences for collaboration and mutual learning. As Senge (1990) describes it, a learning organisation is one that is continually expanding its capacity to create its future. Katz and Earl (2010) claim that in successful networks the focus is on creating the conditions to support individual and collective learning. Building capacity depends on intentionally fostering and developing the opportunities for members to examine their existing beliefs and challenge what they do against new ideas, new knowledge, new skills, and even new dispositions (Stoll, Fink, & Earl, 2003). When networks are focussed on learning, they intentionally seek out and/or create supporting activities, people and opportunities to push them beyond the status quo within their school and network development.

12.6 Continuing Professional Development

A factor that is strongly related to capacity building is professional development. Professional development was found to be the key common element of successful networks in the Curee systematic review (2005). CPD in these networks was often collaborative and in many cases involved external agencies or facilitators. Activities included shared learning experiences, which were often repeated at regular intervals, collaborative meetings, action research projects, and peer teams providing mutual support. Similarly, in our own recent study, CPD was found to be an important part of successful network activity (Ainscow et al., 2006). Again, there appears to be a reciprocal relationship here, in that CPD both facilitates and is facilitated by networking. On the one hand, certain forms of CPD, especially those to do with developing leadership and networking skills, appear to help develop effective collaboration. On the other hand, as we saw in Chapter 9, networking can allow schools to develop more extensive CPD approaches thanks to efficiencies of scale.

Face-to-face interaction appears to be important to the effectiveness of these collaborative activities, and is the main way through which innovation and knowledge are transferred. ICT does not appear to be a key factor, though this may have more to do with the way it has been used in many school-to-school collaborations rather than its potential, which is surely great (Curee, 2005).

12.7 Time Constraints

Time is a key factor in that most studies and evaluations find that, as with any other educational intervention, time needs to be provided in order for networking to be effective. This is particularly important here as networking often leads to a greater burden on staff directly involved, in particular at the deputy or assistant head and middle manager levels. This can lead to resentment, especially where the immediate benefits for the school and the individual are not apparent. Lack of time and increased workload are therefore two key complaints among staff involved in networks (Lindsay et al., 2005). A typical complaint is that it is hard to make any time for collaborative activities in a crowded school calendar, though as has been found in other evaluations (e.g. Harris et al., 2001) the most effective schools appear to be able to find flexible solutions for this problem through rescheduling and optimal use of existing resources. Giving the network enough time to develop is also crucial in developing the trust and shared language needed to make it work.

12.8 Ending Collaboration

Finally, it is important to point out that ending a network arrangement can be a necessary process, but also a difficult one if there is no inbuilt obsolescence to the arrangement. It is important to realise that networks exist for a purpose. They are not there as a goal in themselves. This means that if networks fulfil their purposes, there is a need to reevaluate the value of them. This is even more the case where the network for whatever reason fails to reach its goals. Organisational inertia means that school leaders may fail to properly evaluate whether networks they are part of are still serving a useful purpose. This, however, is an essential activity as network membership may become dysfunctional. However, as Neil Sedaka has pointed out, breaking up is hard to do. Firstly, there is the psychological side of breaking the relationship which can lead to an emotional response from the 'spurned' partner (Nooteboom, 2004) Then, depending on the depth of the relationship, breaking it may lead to a loss due to the loss of particular competencies or capacities. This is particularly the case where the network has come together in order to complement each others' weaknesses, such as in an arrangement where different A-level subjects are offered in different schools. Breaking the relationship could then mean that these subjects cannot be offered. Leaders also need to take into account the effort and cost of setting up a new network following the break up of a previous one (Beije, 1998).

12.9 Conclusion

In summary, then, the internal conditions for effective networking are as follows:

- The development of a sense of collective responsibility for bringing about improvements in all the partner organisations;
- The identification of common improvement priorities that are seen to be relevant to a wide range of stakeholders;
- The development of trusting relationships between schools and key actors;
- The building of sufficient capacity for collaboration, through developing distributed leadership and targeted CPD activities; and
- The establishment of clear and extensive communication channels.

In our view, the absence of such conditions will mean that attempts to encourage teachers and schools to work together are likely to result in little more than time-consuming meetings, which sooner or later will be seen as ineffective and discontinued. This conclusion is, in itself, important for future national initiatives that seek to invest resources in the notion of schools working together in partnerships or networks. Strategies for developing these conditions—or fostering their development at the local level—will be an important determinant of the success such initiatives can expect.

Chapter 13
Successful Networking: External Conditions

As well as internal conditions, it is important that the right external conditions exist for networks of schools to be successful. Our research has identified a number of such conditions.

13.1 External Factors That Enhance Trust

As mentioned in Chapter 12, a prime factor in effective networking and collaboration is the development of relations of trust between schools. This can be easier where schools have a prior relationship to one another, for example because they work together within a school district and key staff know one another through district meetings, where they are part of system of feeder schools, or where they are physically close. Some prior commonality between partners is essential for networks to be successful. This commonality can take a number of forms, such as shared ideological background and values (e.g. networks between schools sharing the same religious denomination), or a need to confront similar issues such as in networks between schools facing challenging circumstances. This commonality is important if the posited sharing and learning are to occur. As Nooteboom (2004) has pointed out, without a shared vocabulary and understanding genuine dialogue is unlikely to emerge, due to the different cognitive reality that organisations may inhabit and the different understandings of reality this entails. However, while shared language is indeed important, it is equally important that this goes alongside shared meanings of concepts, especially where educational jargon is used that may mask a multitude of meanings (e.g. the term distributed leadership). Likewise, the context-specificity of much of the knowledge base on school improvement means that schools that are too different may not be able to contribute much to one another (Chapman & Allen, 2005; Ainscow & West, 2005).

While commonality is important, lack of competition between schools is also seen as a facilitator of effective networking between schools. If competition is strong, the trust that is key to effective networking will not be present (Chapman & Allen, 2005). This has meant that many schools choose to network with partners outside their own catchment area, that are not competing with them for students, notwithstanding the practical difficulties this may entail. The issue of trust comes

D. Muijs et al., *Collaboration and Networking in Education*,
DOI 10.1007/978-94-007-0283-7_13, © Springer Science+Business Media B.V. 2011

to the fore here again, in that where trust between local schools is strong it has been found possible to develop local partnerships and links. This also appears easier where networking is voluntary, as pre-existing relations of trust tend to be stronger. In some ways this finding contradicts some of the work done in the Business studies field, where competing organisations have been found to forge effective networks. These tend to be relatively short-term, and focussed around specific projects, but there is no theoretical reason why similar networks couldn't work in the education sector.

13.2 The Role of Network Brokers

Where collaboration is hindered by a lack of trust or competitive pressures, it can be particularly important to have a network broker or organiser on board. This network broker is typically not someone with a prior relationship with one of the schools and not others, and may be either someone who has worked with all schools in the network, as may be the case for local district personnel, or someone who hasn't worked with any, as may be the case for external consultants. What is particularly important is that the coordinator is seen as an honest broker who is not allied to any of the schools and will not show favour. The role of the coordinator is manifold. S/he often plays an important part in the setting up of the network (see below), and thereafter remains a key person in the network. Her/his role is usually twofold:

- Organisationally, s/he will play a key part in facilitating meeting and activities, coordinating joint actions and plans, and ensuring that regular action takes place so the network doesn't lose impetus.
- Internally, her/his role is to defuse tensions between collaborating schools, ensuring that misunderstandings are corrected and ironed out. S/he will also facilitate the smooth running of the network.

The role of the network broker or organiser can be especially important in those cases where it is an external organisation, such as the local authority or a government agency, that is the main impetus for the collaborative network to be set up. In the latter case there is a need for the broker to think carefully about suitable set-up strategies. A number of options exist:

- A common option, used frequently by government and its agencies, is to provide a monetary incentive for the setting up of the network. This is often a useful way of convincing schools and partners to network, but is far less effective when it comes to sustaining the network. In many cases networks founded on monetary incentives can lead to little more than lip-service to networking, and can quickly fade once the money is gone. This does not mean that there is no role for monetary incentives in the setting up of networks. In particular, some support in covering set-up costs and possible buy-in of external expertise can smooth the process and acceptance of networks among schools. However, one needs to be careful not to create a situation where the monetary reward becomes the sole motivation for networking, and plans and actions need careful monitoring. A bidding process can help, as can the requirement to build post-funding sustainability into any plans to ensure funding.

- A second role brokers can take is to convince possible partners of the benefits of collaboration. Here it is key to speak the language of participating groups, understand their needs and priorities and what they can get out of a collaboration. Values and beliefs are as important here as any material or practical gains, and can often prove the catalyst to collaboration. In education, ideas such as doing the best for all children in the area or authority may prove a strong uniting factor between schools that may otherwise perceive each other as competitors. An appeal to commonly held values and beliefs is therefore often helpful at this stage.
- Providing resources to bring people together is another key brokering role in the set-up phase of networks. In many cases this can take the form of simple practical arrangements like office space for meetings and funding of supply teachers to replace participants in their schools. ICT networking capacity and systems can also be provided, and providing administrative support and brokering can also be effective in getting collaboration off to a successful start (Goldsmith & Eggers, 2004).

13.3 Accountability

One of the main problems for a lot of school networks and for collaboration between schools in general lies in the way accountability mechanisms in many countries have been designed. Typically, accountability is focussed on the individual school, be it in the form of national tests and the publication of school 'league tables' or in the form of inspection, which again has traditionally focussed on the individual school.

This is clearly a barrier to collaboration, especially where it is area-based. As schools are not judged on the results of collaboration, they may be less interested in engaging in it. There is therefore a need to develop accountability mechanisms that can take into account the level of integration that networks of schools may have. Joint submission of school achievement data would be an obvious step, as would joint inspections of school networks, something (the latter, not the former) that is starting to happen in England.

An interesting development in chains of schools in particular is the strong growth of internal forms of accountability. Overarching governing organisations are putting into place monitoring and inspection systems that collect data on the effectiveness of each school in the network in terms of performance and processes, which in some cases have led to head teachers and troubleshooters from the network being put into turn around schools perceived as failing (Chapman, Muijs, & West, 2009). There is also an increased standardisation of procedures in some of these networks of federations, which is followed up by internal inspections and standard operating procedures. Once chains of schools are set up, the necessity to protect the 'brand' makes the setting up of such internal mechanisms inevitable, leading to a powerful form of accountability in such schools which may make effectiveness more likely. Of course, this internal accountability does not preclude collective accountability. Just as a company would present overall results, but monitor the individual performances of its franchises, a chain of academies could in principle be collectively accountable in terms of school performance and inspection data, while maintaining strong internal accountability mechanisms.

In multiagency networks the accountability issue becomes more complicated. Who exactly is responsible for what, in particular aspects of child welfare? This issue has come to the fore in a number of cases of child neglect where different agencies responsible for child welfare have been found not to act with sufficient speed or effectiveness, and where coordination between networks has been lacking. A blame game often results in these situations, and, in England at least, additional regulation has followed, though whether this has had the desired effect is unclear. A particular problem is that what follows is often an overly intrusive regime of inspection and bureaucracy from government and its agencies, which leads to risk-averse and conservative behaviour from partners in a network. This, while understandable from the viewpoint of politicians who tend to receive a lot of the blame whenever anything goes wrong, is a highly undesirable consequence, which goes against one of the key aims of networking, developing innovative solutions. A better approach is to work around a target-setting approach, where each organisation in the network agrees on individual goals and targets that are carefully aligned with overall network goals. This process therefore starts with agreement about what services the network wants to provide, and what the contribution of each individual organisation to these overall goals is. These targets and goals need to be clear and specific, but organisations need to be given flexibility in how to achieve them, without setting up detailed procedures that people need to follow and over-prescribing the details of how organisations should work (Goldsmith & Eggers, 2004). These targets need to be measurable and auditable if accountability is to be effective. It may be helpful to attach incentives to the reaching of particular outcomes as well, though in many cases public sector accountancy rules (which may, for example, prohibit carry-over of surpluses) are extremely unhelpful in this regard and lead to inefficiency and waste. Linking management bonuses and organisational rewards to the achievement of targets is another useful way of aligning organisational and network goals, though practical difficulties of doing this in schools and public sector organisations (such as Union opposition and regulations) are strong. However, as networks can, should and do evolve, it is essential that goals and targets are frequently reviewed in the light of new knowledge, practices, and goals as well as innovation emerging in a network.

Goldsmith and Eggers (2004) recommend using adaptive management techniques to solve the dilemmas posed by multiagency accountability. The concept of adaptive management is flexible with regard to not just methods, but goals as well, and focuses primarily on continuous system monitoring. Continuous feedback and evaluation characterise adaptive management systems, which use this data to change procedures and management systems as necessary. It is a system based on learning through doing that does, however, require continual updating of information, monitoring of said information, and acting upon it. The model is based on testing hypotheses based on best available evidence about what strategies are likely to achieve desired outcomes, clearly and continually documenting processes and outcomes, and adapting the strategies and hypotheses based on this information. While this has worked well in a number of sectors, not least environmental conservation and management, it is complex with regard to data collection, and requires a lot of management and monitoring if it is to work, and may thus be overly complex for a lot of educational networks.

13.4 Partner Motivations

A factor which is likely to affect the success of otherwise of networking is the motivation of the network partners in becoming part of the network. Three main types of motivation can be distinguished:

- Moral altruism, where partners become engaged in networking primarily out of a desire to pursue the public good;
- Enlightened self-interest, where partners collaborate because they feel collaboration will help them to fulfil the goals of their organisation more effectively or efficiently, or in some cases that they can further individual career goals; and
- Concern about being left out, leading them to miss an opportunity or run the risk of becoming politically marginalised (Lawson, 2004).

There is no fixed rule that any of these goals is more or less likely to lead to successful collaboration. However, what is clear is that conflicting goals among partners are likely to store up the potential for future conflict and mistrust and can seriously harm the potential success and existence of the network. It is therefore important to develop a clear understanding of goals of network partners at the outset, and to work through any misunderstandings that may occur, again a network broker can play a key role here, not least in bringing together partners with a compatible vision and goals. There are also some differences in terms of the approach to take to building the network dependent on partner motivations. Where partners are motivated by self-interest there will be a greater need for clear contractual arrangements at the outset. Of course, a strict division of motivations often doesn't accurately reflect the situation. In many cases motivations will be mixed, with elements of altruism and self-interest present simultaneously in network partners.

13.5 The Role of the Local Authority

While in some cases networks have been seen as a replacement for local authority structures, it is still hard to conceive of a way for collaboration to continue as a central element of effective school improvement strategies, without some form of local coordination. As we have seen, in some instances the contributions of LEA officers advisers were significant in the development of the work of collaboratives. Specifically, LEA staff were seen to support and challenge schools in relation to an agreed set of purposes, while head teachers shared the overall management of improvement efforts in their schools.

This sheds insights on the sorts of roles that LEA staff need to take on: *not* managing and leading change, but rather working in partnership with senior people in schools to strengthen collaborative ways of working. In such contexts they can bring specific challenges which derive from their knowledge of the bigger picture across their authority and a clarity of purpose in terms of where the process is heading. At the same time, they can help to broker the sharing of resources and expertise. However, the changes in stance and practice that this implies will be very challenging to the existing thinking of many experienced LEA staff. Consequently, they too will need professional development opportunities that will assist them in rethinking their ways of working.

Beyond the collaboration between schools, there is a need to reach out to others who have an interest in the education of children and young people. In particular, it is important to ensure that parents/carers, elected members, governors, and local community agencies and organisations are aware of, and feel confident about, the new thinking about school improvement, with its emphasis on collaboration. In this respect, the moves towards the integration of support staff from different agencies within district structures that are occurring in some parts of the country, are a very helpful development.

While our conclusions are generally very positive, there is still much to be done if the somewhat uneven progress that has been achieved across the country can be turned to even greater effect. As we have argued, this will require shared leadership across all levels of the service, particularly at the local level.

This confirms other research that shows how what goes on at the district level has a significant role to play in respect to processes of school improvement. It implies the negotiation of new, inter-dependent relationships between schools, LEAs and their wider communities. Introducing such an approach in the current context, with its cocktail of competing agendas and confusion about forms of governance, is, however, far from straightforward.

In our view, national policy makers would be naive to overlook the influence of what happens at the local authority level, particularly in urban districts. Local history, inter-connections between schools, and established relationships are always there, helping to shape what happens, even if they are overlooked. Consequently, levers need to be found that will be powerful in encouraging the development of inter-dependence among groups of schools within districts. In this way further progress can be made towards a national education system that is geared to raising standards for all students, in all schools, through the systematic orchestration and, sometimes, the redistribution of available resources and expertise.

Through our own work, we have tried to identify factors at the local level that have the potential to either facilitate or inhibit such collaborative moves among schools. Our research suggests that two factors, particularly when they are closely linked, seem to be super-ordinate to all others. These are: *clarity of purpose*, and *the forms of evidence* that are used to measure educational performance.

Enhancing clarity of purpose through a well-orchestrated debate about values and priorities can have leverage in respect to fostering the conditions within which groups of schools feel encouraged to collaborate in achieving common purposes. Such a debate needs to involve all stakeholders within a local community, including politicians and, indeed, the media. It must also involve those within the local education department so that they have clarity as to what must drive their actions. What the experiences summarised in these notes suggest is that such debate need not take place in the abstract. Rather, opportunities to pursue the debate can be sought and taken within what have become the everyday processes of school improvement.

Our search for 'levers' for improvement has also led us to acknowledge the importance of evidence. In essence, it leads us to conclude that, within education systems, 'what gets measured gets done'. So, for example, LEAs are required to collect far more statistical data than ever before. This is widely recognised as a double-edged sword precisely because it is such a potent lever for change. Data are required in order to monitor the progress of children, evaluate the impact of interventions, enable review of the effectiveness of policies and processes, plan new initiatives, and so on. In these senses, data can, justifiably, be seen as the life-blood of continuous improvement.

All of this suggests that great care needs to be exercised in deciding what evidence is collected and, indeed, how it is used. LEAs are required by Government to collect particular data. Given national policies, they cannot opt out of collecting such data on the grounds that their publication might be misinterpreted, or that they may influence practice in an unhelpful way. On the other hand, LEAs and schools are free to collect additional evidence that can then be used to evaluate the effectiveness of their own policy and practice in respect to progress towards greater equity within the system. The challenge for LEAs is, therefore, to work with schools to harness the potential of evidence as a lever for change, while avoiding the problems described earlier.

All of this suggests that the UK Government's current emphasis on the creation of 'independent specialist schools' needs to be handled sensitively, if it is not to further disadvantage schools and groups of learners who already underachieving. While it is true that, by and large, schools improve as a result of leadership from the inside, it is also the case that the wider context influences the progress of such improvement efforts, for good or ill. This is the power of what we have characterised as 'inter-dependence'. It leads us to argue that while, in order to improve, schools do have to become more autonomous and self-improving; at the same time, it draws our attention to the way that neighbouring schools can add value to one another's efforts.

Continuing with the search for powerful levers, then, we believe that it will be helpful to those at the local level who are encouraging schools to collaborate if national policy initiatives continue to emphasise the principle of collaboration as being a fundamental element of efforts to raise standards across the education system; and, remembering that 'what gets measured gets done', regulatory frameworks must pay due attention to this same principle. In our view this is the way *to get schools to operate as part of a network to deliver a fully comprehensive education.*

13.6 Conclusion

In summary, then, the internal conditions for effective networking are as follows:

- External help from credible consultants/advisers (from the local authority or elsewhere) who also have the disposition and confidence to learn alongside their school-based partners.
- A willingness and desire among local authority staff to support and engage with the collaborative process, exploring and developing new roles and relationships.
- The presence of incentives that encourage key stakeholders to explore the possibility that collaboration will be in their own interests.
- Suitable motivation for collaboration between partners.
- An accountability system than encourages, rather than discourages, collaboration.

It is therefore clear that for collaboration and networking to flourish, policy makers at both local and national levels have an important role to play. While collaboration has and will exist in adverse external conditions, as a systemic school improvement model which we believe has great potential, it does require policy support in the areas mentioned above.

Chapter 14
Leading Networks

Despite the growth of networks and collaboration both in education and in the public sector more generally, most of what we know about management derives from studies of single organisations. This is clearly problematic in the light of observed differences in the nature of networks. Leading networks requires an additional skills set, focussed on organising resources and partners, and, not least, their relationships, something which head teachers have not traditionally had to do to this extent.

14.1 The Role of the Head Teacher

The role of the head teacher or principal is a key one in networks. We have seen in many of our case studies that successful networks either originate from the initiative of one or more charismatic head teachers, or else are steered through the always difficult set-up phase by individual leaders. While, therefore, we have evidence that distributed leadership is fostered through collaboration and networking, it remains the case that strong head teacher leadership at the network level appears to be a facet of many successful networks. There is evidence both from education and from other field that leaders play a key role in the establishment of networks, McGuire and Agranoff (2007), for example, pointing to the fact that a leader or leaders usually lie at the basis on new public service networks. Within schools themselves, head teachers and other senior staff in schools who are willing and able to drive collaboration forward are key to making it work. As with other educational interventions, networking will only work if head teachers are committed and behind the idea. Head teacher support is necessary to encourage other school staff to see network activities as key, to put in train the cultural and structural changes needed for collaborative work with other schools or organisations, and, not least, to ensure that time is freed up for staff to take part in network activities (for example joint CPD with another school) and that staff are encouraged to disseminate the outcomes of any network activity in the school. Obviously, where a network proposes thoroughgoing forms of integration such as teachers teaching at multiple schools or joint appointments the role of the head in making this happen is crucial. Head teacher leadership is therefore clearly important to effective networking (Lindsay et al., 2005). At the

D. Muijs et al., *Collaboration and Networking in Education*,
DOI 10.1007/978-94-007-0283-7_14, © Springer Science+Business Media B.V. 2011

individual school level, this means that the Senior Management Teams of all network schools need to support the network in order for it to be sustainable. Networks that are driven solely by staff lower down the school hierarchy, while potentially successful in the short term, are unlikely to show long-term sustainability. Networks of teachers, where there is little senior management involvement, are unlikely to result in systemic change across the school and are likely to peter out (Ainscow & West, 2005; Harris et al., 2005). In practice, according to Hadfield (2007), most successful networks are driven by a small group of activist leaders, given 'permission to lead' by colleagues. According to one report, firm directive leadership is required at the start, at least for schools facing challenging circumstances, which can later be relaxed. A more distributed approach can then be adopted once changes have been bedded in Chapman and Harris (2004). Changing leadership styles can be fraught with difficulty; however, as staff expectations may have become embedded to the extent that such changes may be met by mistrust and a reluctance to take on new leadership roles (Muijs & Harris, 2003).

14.2 Other Leadership Roles in a Network

As well as leadership by head teachers, we typically find a number of other important leadership roles in most successful networks.

A key role in the leadership of networks is played by so-called *boundary spanners*, staff members with a specific role in integrating the work of different organisations (Nylen, 2007). These boundary spanners may occupy a variety of positions in the organisational hierarchy of their 'home' organisation, and don't necessarily have to be senior. Their role tends to be particularly crucial at the start of collaboration and during problems, where their understanding of issues in the different collaborating schools can lead to them being ideal brokers. Boundary spanners therefore illustrate the importance of distributed leadership in networks, being typical of roles that are both typically distributed by heads to colleagues lower down the school hierarchy, while the role itself will develop the leader and is an important one to successful collaboration.

Another network leadership role is that of *network designer* or designers. This can be a head teacher or group of head teachers, an external broker, or a Local Authority officer, but needs to be someone with a strategic vision of how the network will function and what its goals are going to be. The key role of the network designer occurs at the start-up phase. The job of the network designer is, with goals and capacities clearly in mind, to identify appropriate network partners, make contact and bring all partners around the table to discuss forms and function of the network. The network designer needs to communicate expectations of how the network will function and what its goals are, and choose an appropriate network design. Again, this is clearly a task that will need to be undertaken in close collaboration with network partners and that will usually be more of a brokering role than a hierarchical management function (except in those cases where the network is clearly top-down) (Goldsmith & Eggert, 2004). Research has shown that most educational networks have a de facto network designer, in that it tends to be an individual or a small group of individuals, usually at the senior management level, who take the initiative to start up a network and subsequently tend to be the key actors within the network (Muijs, 2008). However, formalising this role may in some cases be beneficial, especially where a network contains a large number of (potential) partners, as doing so will create clarity and clear structures of responsibility. In his review of leadership in Networked Learning Communities in England, Hadfield (2007) identified three key steps in the setting up of networks which were, in this case, led by head teachers. The first stage is courting, where the leading school(s) approach potential partners and develop proposals for network activity. During this phase heads contact other schools and sometimes make links with other networks. During the second 'aligning' phase, leadership buy-in is sought from schools contacted during the courting phase, through a sometimes extensive process of negotiation. Concrete network plans are drawn up. In the third, connecting and embedding phase, the network is formalised by creating links between schools and opportunities for teachers to work together.

Once the network is up and running the role of *network coordinator* becomes important. This is an aspect that is often missing in educational networks. In many cases, it is left to meetings of head teachers to do the coordination. This may work for a while, but leaves the network highly vulnerable to changes in staffing at the senior management level, to issues that may take the eye of particular school leaders off collaboration, such as being put into special measures (a category of failing school used by the English government). It can also happen that misunderstandings occur between head teachers, or that politicking and rivalry between schools and heads may weaken the work of the coordinating team. Therefore, it can be helpful to appoint a coordinator who is responsible for the network rather than individual schools. There are different models for this. In some federations, as we saw earlier, an *executive head* with responsibility for the federation as a whole rather than individual schools is appointed, which in effect puts an extra layer of overarching management above that of the schools. A joint governing body may do some of the coordination, but day-to-day coordination work cannot usually be done at this level and is not typically the role of a governing body. Many schools don't want to go as far as having a joint executive head. In that case other coordinating mechanisms are possible. In some cases a deputy head or other senior manager from one of the schools takes on this role, but the risk of a viewpoint that is too strongly associated with one particular school remains. In other cases an external coordinator takes on this role, usually the external broker of the network. This has the advantage of providing an impartial voice with regards to the individual schools, which can therefore promote greater trust. Arranging meetings requires long-term planning, and is more difficult the larger the cluster group. The network coordinator can also help to solve the problem of the time it may take for head teachers and senior leaders to travel to meetings, especially where the network serves a large geographical area, as is the case in many rural collaboratives, or where the network is not geographically based, as in some of the federations of academies. This problem can be reduced by holding fewer, longer meetings and/or by forming subgroups for specific projects, or the network coordinator can coordinate meetings and events, and timetables between schools (Jones, 2009).

14.3 Characteristics of Successful Leadership in Networks

Leaders' interpersonal skills are another aspect of successful networking. Inevitably, networking entails the bringing together of different organisational cultures, so some measure of misalignment and misunderstanding is inevitable. In order to be able to overcome this problem, a good understanding of their strengths and weaknesses and the emotional impact of collaboration are necessary (Muijs, 2006b). Heads also need to be open and honest, in order to help develop the trust that is so important to effective networking arrangements.

However, as well as these softer elements of management, networks appear most successful where a clear management structure exists (Lindsay et al., 2005). Again, this is similar to findings from other studies on school effectiveness and school improvement, which have, for example, shown that even school improvement based on notions of distributed leadership benefits from strong and clear management structures (Muijs & Harris, 2007). In some of the federations, the creation of new management posts at the network level (such as Associate Heads and Assistant Heads for the whole federation) has been found to aid that process, though this would only be appropriate where the network is intended to show permanence rather than a more short-term focus on particular programmes or aspects of improvement. New roles, described by Fullan (2004) as 'system leadership' are emerging in networks, largely structured around key brokering roles. These include the building of group identity, trust, and the fostering of mutual knowledge.

More generally, there is evidence that networks not only require additional leadership roles and skills, but that they, by creating these, help to involve more school staff in leadership, thus promoting both distributed leadership and an increased leadership capacity in the system. Likewise, the creation of leadership roles specifically related to network leadership creates a cadre of people with experience of system leadership, and thus makes future networking easier (Hadfield, 2007; Fullan, 2004).

One of the key differences between managing networks and single organisations is the fact that networks are generally voluntary collaborations between equals, as opposed to hierarchical organisations. This is a very different situation than the norm for educational managers, used to being at the top of a hierarchical system, where, essentially, what they say goes. When managing a network, the role becomes very different, focussed on getting a community of equals (who are likely to jealously guard that sense of equality and strongly resist signs of hierarchy) to work together and coordinate activities for the common good. This is what is known by economists as the Joint Production Problem. This form of management is characterised by the lack of possible sanctions, and by often limited economic incentives (Milward & Provan, 2003). As Handy (1991) pointed out, the good thing for network managers is that they manage a programme with far greater resources in terms of staff, but the bad thing is that none of them think they work for you.

According to some theories, networks are in fact unmanageable, due to the fact that they emerge from multiple micro-interactions, and therefore are not controlled by any one actor (Ritter et al., 2003). This view of networking fits well with a 'new social movements' perspective, but does not fit well with those networks that have been more deliberately created, and where often a network leadership position has been formally created, in which cases some element of network management is present. What is clear is that in many cases some form of central administration and management is necessary for a network to be sustainable and effective over time (Milward & Provan, 2003).

Being perceived as an honest broker is key to effective network management, and to the building up of the necessary credibility as leader. This is closely linked to the importance of managing relationships. Management of relationships for individual organisations has been hypothesised as containing a number of key elements, such as cooperation, communication and involvement (Ling-Yee & Ogunmokun, 2001). Managing a range of relationships involves planning (developing a relationship strategy), organising (implementing the plan, staffing (who deals with what aspects of the relationship) and controlling (i.e. reviewing the results of the collaboration) (Ritter et al., 2003).

Consensus building has been identified as another key role within networks, and one that is part of the role of all head teachers in a network. In his study, Hadfield (2007) found that in the early stages of network development the aspect of consensus building that was central was the selection of an initial theme that could give cohesion to the work of the network as a whole. Later on consensus building emerged around the choice of specific network activities.

Continuous change and fluidity of networks is another issue managers have to be able to deal with, and this necessitates a flexible outlook and, again, strong communication skills. Communication in particular is important, as the more diffuse nature of a network can mean that not all teachers and other staff will be clear on network goals and purposes. Continuous and extensive communication to staff is therefore imperative. Likewise, parents may not be clear on the benefits of networking. In particular, where a highly effective school starts to collaborate with a school perceived as less effective there are often tensions with parents who fear that their head may lose focus on their school and pupils. Communication with parents is therefore important (Jones, 2009).

14.4 Distribution and Devolution of Leadership in Networks

An additional complication is that leaders of networks in education usually still have a dual role, that of leader of the network and that of leader of their school. This can cause problems, as effective network managers need to be aware of structures, actions, and developments in all the schools in the network, not just their own. They need to develop a management style in which it becomes equally normal for them to spend time in partner schools as in their own schools, and develop a culture in which this is an expectation of leaders in those school as well as the network leaders' own school.

A related problem is the fact that in many cases leaders of networks are no longer able to play a strong instructional leadership role due to the additional responsibilities of leading the network. This is problematic in a number of ways. Firstly, leadership research clearly shows instructional leadership to be a strong correlate of school effectiveness (Hallinger, 2003). Secondly both effectiveness and improvement research show that what happens in the classroom is the central factor in improving pupil outcomes, and thus something that a successful network will have to attend to (Muijs & Reynolds, 2002). Finally, if the network head was, as head of her school, previously the key instructional leader within the school that role may be lost. There are two main solutions to this problem. Firstly, distributed leadership where the instructional leadership role is shared across schools and the network may alleviate the pressure on the individual leader to fulfil this role on her own. That this does happen is clear from a number of studies that have shown that the number of middle leaders increases substantially in networks, and that they are typically engaged in leading network-related activities (Hadfield, 2007). Secondly, it is often sensible to devolve some management and leadership tasks to other leaders in the organisation. One interesting development in this regard is the increasing use of School Business Managers in networks and federations of schools. School Business Managers are typically from an administrative background, but are given senior management responsibilities in areas such as finance, procurement, and buildings management. They take part in Senior Leadership Team meetings and are part of the senior management team. In England, specific qualifications and training exists aimed at developing administrative staff to take on these roles through a step approach that includes a certificate, diploma, and advanced diploma in School Business Management. Evaluations point to positive impacts of having School Business Managers trained and responsible in this way, and networks of schools benefit particularly in terms of the School Business Manager taking on roles for which school leaders may feel less well prepared (Muijs et al., 2010).

14.5 Conclusion

From the above it should be evident, firstly, that leadership is every bit as important to networks as it has been found to be for individual schools, and that many of the characteristics of effective leaders in schools carry over into effective network leadership. Factors such as distributing leadership, developing school climate, and shaping goals are all factors in effective leadership at any level. However, there are also a number of more specific skills and behaviours, or at least skills and behaviours that become more central, when leading in a network. Working in a horizontal rather vertical hierarchical context, brokering, and collaborative skills all become far more important to network leadership than they are to the leadership of individual schools. Networks also tend to lead to their own additional leadership roles, such as network coordinators.

What is clear in all this is that, while schools may be improved quite rapidly, developing networks takes time, and networks need to be given the time and stability to develop. Change should occur incrementally (Milward & Provan, 2003). This is linked to the need for leaders to build up legitimacy with partner organisations that does not necessarily exist to the same extent as in their own organisation, where it is in part a function of the position of power the manager has. Legitimacy can grow as partners get to know the manager and the network shows itself to be more than just an ephemeral phenomenon.

Chapter 15
Some Final Thoughts

As Hopkins and Reynolds (2001) have stated, school improvement as a field has gone through four main phases. The first phase is described as being characterised by unsystematic attempts at improvement and an emphasis on organisational change and school self-evaluation. Fragmented and weak implementation and a lack of connection to student outcomes were seen as problems with this approach. The second phase was characterised by a rapprochement between school improvement and school effectiveness. School effectiveness contributed its knowledge base and value-added methodologies, while school improvement had developed stronger implementation strategies. Hopkins and Reynolds then posit a third phase, which emphasises student outcomes, classroom processes, and capacity building, as well as sophisticated professional development approaches. Though successes can clearly be identified, the extent to which third phase approaches have led to systemic improvement is debatable, leading to a search for 'fourth phase' approaches. One thing that is clear in the description of the first three phases is that they are generally predicated on individual schools working with school improvers, buying-into school improvement programmes, or at most collectively participating in a programme. What is not strongly articulated in these three phases is the idea of school-to-school collaboration as a key motor for school improvement. This is not due to a lack of activity in this area, as in recent years there has been a strong impetus towards collaboration between schools as a road to improvement, and as this book has shown, there are some compelling examples of success. Is it therefore possible that practice has already moved to a fourth phase of school improvement based on collaboration, while academic writing and research has yet to catch up?

Whether this is the case is, at present, still debatable, as we do not as yet have enough quantitative evidence on impact, and there are distinct national differences with regard to the extent to which networking and collaboration between schools has become a central paradigm and practice in school improvement and educational reform.

What is clear, however, is that there is an overall increase in interest in collaboration and networking as a possible school improvement strategy, and one that has been officially encouraged in many areas, not least England. It is therefore certainly timely to draw together theoretical perspectives and empirical evidence as we have attempted to do in this book.

D. Muijs et al., *Collaboration and Networking in Education*,
DOI 10.1007/978-94-007-0283-7_15, © Springer Science+Business Media B.V. 2011

Theoretical perspectives are of particular importance in this area which, certainly in education, has often remained under-theorised. Therefore, Part I of this book focussed specifically on theoretical perspectives of networking and collaboration, highlighting some of the implications for practice of these theoretical orientations. This part of the book is also an invitation to researchers, practitioners, and policy makers to think more clearly about the goals of collaboration and what these may mean for the way networks are set up and managed.

In Part II, a number of empirical studies were introduced on different types of networking and collaboration. Overall, not only do these examples provide clear evidence of the potential of collaboration for organisational improvement, but they also make clear that this is by no means a given. Each chapter in this part points to caveats and examples where collaboration has been less successful as well as to the successes. That is why in Part III we have tried to bring together some of the evidence we have on what internal, external, and leadership factors can enhance network effectiveness.

In their different ways, all of this book presents evidence of the potential of networking and collaboration as a way of improving schools, not just in terms of standards but in terms of equity as well. However, we would also suggest that networking is by no means a panacea for school improvement. Clarity on goals and changes in culture and attitudes, structures, and incentives are required for collaborative strategies to work. Is networking then the fourth phase in school improvement? That is probably an overstatement of the case in a world in which a variety of approaches from school vouchers to extended schools co-exist and compete as new school improvement models; but in our opinion networking is certainly one of the more promising developments in education today, and one that deserves support from policy makers and school improvers, alongside other promising approaches such as strategies to tackle within-school variation (Reynolds, 2007) and approaches that are focussed on effective pedagogical strategies such as peer learning and small group work (Chapman et al., 2009), and should be considered as part of a menu of school improvement strategies.

We hope this book has proved thought-provoking and enlightening.

References

Abbott-Chapman, J., & Kilpatrick, S. (2001). Improving post-school outcomes for rural school leavers. *Australian Journal of Education, 45*(1), 35–47.

Abrams, L., & Gibbs, J. T. (2000). Planning for change: School-community collaboration in a full-service elementary school. *Urban Education, 35*(1), 79–103.

Adler, L. (1995). *The Los Angeles area business/education partnership. A study of the impact of a community based school to work program for high risk youth.* Washington, DC: Educational Information Center (ERIC).

Agranoff, R. (2006). *Managing within networks: Adding value to public organizations.* Washington: Georgetown University Press.

Ahrendt, H. (1968). *Truth and politics between past and future: Eight exercises in political thought.* New York: Viking Press.

Ainscow, M. (1999). *Understanding the development of inclusive schools.* London: Falmer Press.

Ainscow, M., Booth, T., & Dyson, A. (2006). Inclusion and the standards agenda: Negotiating policy pressures in England. *International Journal of Inclusive Education, 10*(4–5), 295–308.

Ainscow, M., Booth, T., Dyson, A., Farrell, P., Frankham, J., Gallannaugh, F., et al. (2006). *Improving schools, developing inclusion.* London: Routledge.

Ainscow, M., Dyson, A., Goldrick, S., & Kerr, K. (2009). Using research to foster inclusion and equity within the context of new labour education reforms. In C. Chapman & H. Gunter (Eds.), *Radical reform: Perspectives on an era of educational change.* London: Routledge.

Ainscow, M., & Howes, A. (2001). *LEAs and school improvement: What is it that makes the difference?* Paper presented at the British Education Research Association Conference, Leeds, September 2001.

Ainscow, M., & Howes, A. (2007). Working together to improve urban secondary schools: A study of practice in one city. *School Leadership and Management, 27*(3), 285–300.

Ainscow, M., Howes, A. J., Farrell, P., & Frankham, J. (2003). Making sense of the development of inclusive practices. *European Journal of Special Needs Education, 18*(2), 227–242.

Ainscow, M., Howes, A., & Tweddle, D. (2006). Making sense of the impact of recent education policies: A study of practice. In M. Ainscow & M. West (Eds.), *Improving urban schools: Leadership and collaboration.* Maidenhead: Open University Press.

Ainscow, M., & Kaplan, I. (2006). Using evidence to encourage inclusive school development: Possibilities and challenges. *Australasian Journal of Special Education, 29*(2), 106–116.

Ainscow, M., Muijs, D., & West, M. (2006). *Improving schools in challenging circumstances: A study of school-to-school collaboration.* Paper presented at the Australian Association for Research in Education Conference, Sidney, Australia, October 2006.

Ainscow, M., & West, M. (2005). *School-to-school collaboration in complex and challenging circumstances.* Paper prepared for the National College for School leadership. Manchester: University of Manchester.

DOI 10.1007/978-94-007-0283-7, © Springer Science+Business Media B.V. 2011

Ainscow, M., & West, M. (2006). *Improving urban schools*. Buckingham: Open University Press.

Airriess, A., Li, W., Leong, K., Chen, A., & Keith, V. (2007). Church-based social capital, networks and geographical scale: Katrina evacuation, relocation, and recovery in a New Orleans Vietnamese American community. *Geoforum, 39*(3), 1333–1346.

Alter, C., & Hage, J. (1993). *Organizations working together*. London: Sage.

Anderson, P. (1999). Complexity theory and organization science. *Organization Science, 10*(3), 216–232.

Anyon, J. (2005). *Radical possibilities. Public policy, urban education and a new social movement*. New York: Routledge.

Atkinson, M., Halsey, K., Kinder, K., & Wilkin, A. (2002). *An evaluation of the devolution of education welfare services in secondary schools*. Slough: NFER.

Becker, H. (1958). Problems of inference and proof in participant observation. *American Sociological Review, 23*, 652–660.

Berkman, L., Glass, T., Brisette, I., & Seeman, T. (2000). From social integration to health: Durkheim in the new millennium. *Social Science and Medicine, 51*, 843–857.

Berry, F. S., Brower, R. S., Choi, S. O., Xinfang Goa, W., Jang, H. S, Kwon, M., et al. (2004). Three traditions of network research: What the public management research agenda can learn from other research communities. *Public Administration Review, 64*(5), 539–552.

Besnard, P. (1988). The true nature of anomie. *Sociological Theory, 6*(1), 91–95.

Bielefeldt, T., Moursund, D., Underwood, S., & Underwood, D. (1999). *Connected learning communities: Findings from the road ahead program, 1995–1997*. Paper presented at the American educational research association annual conference, Montreal, QC, Canada, April 1999.

Blair, T. (1997). *'Bringing Britain together'. Speech by the Prime Minister, the Rt Hon Tony Blair MP Stockwell Park School, South London, Monday 8 December 1997*. London: Social Exclusion Unit.

Blunkett, D. (1999). *Excellence for the many, not just the few: Raising standards and extending opportunities in our schools*. The CBI president's reception address by the Rt. Hon. David Blunkett MP 19 July 1999, London: DfEE.

Borgatti, P., & Cross, R. (2003). A relational view of information seeking and learning in social networks. *Management Science, 49*(4), 432–445.

Borgatti, S., & Foster, P. (2003). The network paradigm in organizational research: A review and typology. *Journal of Management, 29*(6), 991–1013.

Boynton, P., & Cusick, L. (2006). Editorial: Sex workers to pay the price. *British Medical Journal, 332*, 190–191.

Bragg, S., Craig, J., Cunningham, I., Eraut, M., Fielding, M., Gillinson, S., et al. (2004). *Factors influencing the transfer of good practice (report on DfES Project JC154/2001/1.)* Brighton: University of Sussex.

Brashears, M. E. (2010). Anomia and the sacred canopy: Testing a network theory. *Social Networks, 32*(3), 187–196.

Brehony, K. J., & Deem, R. (2003). Education policy. In N. Ellison & C. Pierson (Eds.), *Developments in British social policy 2* (pp. 177–193). Basingstoke: Palgrave Macmillan.

Brown, J. S., & Duguid, P. (2000). *Social life of information*. Boston: Harvard Business School Press.

Bryk, A., & Raudensbusch, D. K. (2002). *Trust in schools*. New York: Russell Sage Foundation.

Buechler, S. M. (1995). New social movement theories. *The Sociological Quarterly, 36*(3), 441–464.

Burt, R. S. (1992). *Structural holes: The social structure of competition*. Cambridge, MA: Harvard University Press.

Busher, H., & Hodgkinson, K. (1996). Co-operation and tension between autonomous schools: A study of inter-school networking. *Educational Review, 48*(1), 55–64.

Cattell, V. (2001). Poor people, poor places, and poor health: The mediating role of social networks and social capital. *Social Science and Medicine, 52*(10), 1501–1516.

Chapman, C., & Ainscow, M. (2007). *Networking for transformation: Making it happen.* Unpublished pamphlet, University of Manchester.

Chapman, C., & Allen, T (2005). *Partnerships for improvement: The specialist schools achievement programme*. London: The Specialist Schools Trust.

Chapman, C., & Fullan, M (2007). Collaboration and partnership for equitable improvement: Towards a networked learning system? *School Leadership and Management, 27*(3), 207–213.

Chapman, C., & Harris, A. (2004). Improving schools in difficult and challenging contexts: Strategies for improvement. *Journal of Education Research, 46*(3), 219–228.

Chapman, C., Muijs, D., & West, M. (2009). *Developing innovative approaches to promote learning: What works and why?* A paper prepared by the effectiveness and improvement research group, school of education, university of Manchester for the greater Manchester challenge, Manchester: University of Manchester, Effectiveness and Improvement Research Group.

Cloke, P. (Ed.). (2003). *Country visions.* London: Pearson.

Cohen, W., & Levithal, D. (1990). Absorptive capacity: A new perspective on learning and innovation. *Administrative Science Quarterly, 35*, 128–152.

Craig, J. (2005). *Taking the wide view. The new leadership of extended schools.* Nottingham: NCSL.

Cummings, C., & Dyson, A. (2007). The role of schools in area regeneration. *Research Papers in Education, 22*(1), 1–22.

Cummings, C., Dyson, A., Muijs, D., Papps, I., Pearson, D., Raffo, C., et al. (2009). *Evaluation of the full-service extended schools initiative. Final report.* London: DfES.

CUREE. (2005). *Systematic research review: The impact of networks on pupils, practitioners, organisations and the committees they serve.* Nottingham: NCSL.

Datnow, A., Hubbard, L., & Mehan, H. (2002). *Extending educational reform: From one school to many.* London: Routledge.

DfEE. (2001). *The code of practice of practice on LEA-school relations*. London: DfES.

DfES. (2003). *Every child matters.* London: The Stationery Office.

DfES. (2006). *Education and Inspections Act 2006.* London: The Stationery Office.

Diani, M. (2003). Networks and social movements: A research programme, In M. Diani & D. McAdam (Eds.), *Social movements and networks: Relational approaches to collective action* (pp. 299–319). Oxford: Oxford University Press.

Dryfoos, J. G. (1995). Full service schools: Revolution or fad? *Journal of Research on Adolescence, 5*(2), 147–172.

Dunn, W. (1983). Social network theory. *Science Communication, 1983*(4), 453–461.

Durkheim, E. (1972). *Selected writings.* Cambridge: Cambridge University Press.

Fielding, M. (1999). Radical collegiality: Affirming teaching as an inclusive professional practice. *Australian Educational Researcher, 26*(2), 1–34.

Finkelstein, N. D., & Grubb, W. N. (2000). Making sense of education and training markets: Lessons from England. *American Educational Research Journal, 37*(3), 601–631.

Freidl, W. (1997). The impact of anomia as a factor in a demand resource model of health. *Social Science and Medicine, 44*(9), 1357–1365.

Fullan, M. (1991). *The new meaning of educational change.* London: Cassell.

Fullan, M. (2004). *Systems thinking in action.* London: DfES/NCSL.

Garrett, R. K. (2006). Protest in an Information Society: A review of literature on social movements and new ICTs. *Information, Communication and Society, 9*(2), 202– 224.

Gettinger, M., Stoiber, K. C., & Lange, J. (1999). Collaborative investigation of inclusive early education practices: A blueprint for teacher researcher partnership. *Journal of Early Intervention, 22*(3), 257–265.

Giroux, H. A., & Schmidt, M. (2004). Closing the achievement gap: A metaphor for children left behind. *Journal of Educational Change, 5*, 213–228.

Glatter, R., & Harvey, J. A. (2006). *Varieties of shared headship: A preliminary exploration.* Nottingham: National College of School Leadership.

Goldsmith, S., & Eggers, W. D. (2004). *Government by network. The new shape of the public sector.* Washington, DC: Brookings Institution Press.

Grant, R. M., Baden-Fuller, C. (2004). A knowledge accessing theory of strategic alliances. *Journal of Management Studies, 41*(1), 61–84.

Greenberg, K. H. (1996, June). *The cognitive enrichment network education model (COGNET).* Paper presented at the 3rd head start national research conference, Washington, DC.

Hadfield, M. (2005, April), *Middle leaders and the nature of distributed leadership in networks.* Paper presented at the American Educational Research Association (AERA) Conference, Montreal.

Hadfield, M. (2007). Co-leaders and middle leaders: The dynamic between leaders and followers in networks of schools. *School Leadership and Management, 27*(3), 259–283.

Hall, V., & Wallace, M. (1993). Collaboration as a subversive activity: A professional response to externally imposed competition between schools? *School Leadership and Management, 13*(2), 110–117.

Hallinger, P. (2003). Leading educational change: Reflections on the practice of instructional and transformational leadership. *Cambridge Journal of Education, 33*(3), 329–352.

Handy, C. (1991). *The age of unreason.* London: London Business Books.

Handy, C. (1994). *The age of paradox.* Boston: Harvard Business School Press.

Hargreaves, A. (2003a). *Teaching in the knowledge society: Education in the age of insecurity.* Buckingham: Open University Press.

Hargreaves, D. H. (2003b). *Education epidemic: Transforming secondary schools through innovation networks.* London: Demos.

Hargreaves, D. H. (2004). *Learning for life.* London: Policy Press.

Hargreaves, L., Comer, C., & Galton, M. (1996). The national curriculum: Can small schools deliver? Confidence and competence levels of teachers in small rural primary schools. *British Educational Research Journal, 22*(1), 89–99.

Harris, A. (2001). Building the capacity for school improvement. *School Leadership & Management, 21*(3), 261–270.

Harris, A., Chapman, C., Muijs, D., Russ, J., & Stoll, L. (2006). Improving schools in challenging contexts: exploring the possible. *School Effectiveness and School Improvement, 17*(4), 409–424.

Harris, A., Hopkins, D., & Wordsworth, J. (2001). The implementation and impact of success for all in English schools. In R. E. Slavin, & N. A. Madden (Eds.), *Success for all: Research and reform in elementary education.* Mahwah, NJ: Erlbaum. ISBN 0 8058 3810-4

Harris, A., & Lambert, L. (2003). *Building leadership capacity for school improvement.* Milton Keynes: Open University Press.

Harris, A., Muijs, D., Chapman, C., Stoll, L., & Russ, J. (2005). Improving schools in challenging circumstances: Exploring the possible. *School Effectiveness and School Improvement, 16*(4), 230–246.

Heclo, H. (1978). Issue networks and the executive establishment. In A. King (Ed.), *The new American political system.* Washington, DC: American Enterprise Institute.

Hiatt-Michael, D. (2003). *Promising practices to connect schools to the community.* Greenwich, CT: Information Age Publishing.

Hopkins, D., Ainscow, M., & West, M. (1994). *School improvement in an era of change.* London: Cassell.

Hopkins, D., & Reynolds, D. (2001). The past, present and future of school improvement: Towards the third age. *British Educational Research Journal, 27*(4), 459–475.

Howes, A., & Ainscow, M. (2006). Collaboration with a city-wide purpose: making paths for sustainable educational improvement. In M. Ainscow & M. West (Eds.), *Improving urban schools: Leadership and collaboration* (pp. 104–116). Buckingham: Open University Press.

Howley, A., Carnes, M., Eldridge, A., Huber, D., Longun, M., Kotler, R., et al. (2005). The poor little rich district: The effects of suburbanization on a rural school and community. *Journal of Research in Rural Education, 20*(9), 1–14.

James, P., St Leger, P., & Ward, K. (2001). *Making connections: The evaluation of the Victorian full service schools program.* Melbourne, VIC: Dept of Education and Training.
Johns, S., Kilpatrick, S., & Loechel, B. (2003, May). *Pathways from rural schools: Does school VET make a difference?* Paper presented at the AVETRA Conference, Canberra.
Jones, J. (2009). The development of leadership capacity through collaboration in small schools. *School Leadership and Management, 29*(2), 129–156.
Kahne, J., O'Brien, J., Brown, A., & Quinn, T. (2001). Leveraging social capital and school improvement: The case of a school network and a comprehensive community initiative in Chicago. *Educational Administration Quarterly, 37*(4), 429–461.
Kannappel, P., & DeYoung, A. (1999). The rural school problem in 1999. A review and critique of the literature. *Journal of Research in Rural Education, 15*(2), 67–79.
Katz, S., & Earl, L. (2010). Learning about networked learning communities. *School Effectiveness and School Improvement, 21*(1), 27–51.
Kotter, J. P. (1998). *Leading change.* Cambridge, MA: Harvard Business School Press.
Lamb, S., & Rumberger, R. (1999). *The initial work and education experiences of early school leavers: A comparative study of Australia and the United States* (Research Report No. 14). Longitudinal Surveys of Australian Youth. Camberwell: Australian Council for Educational Research.
Latour, B. (2005). *Reassembling the social.* New York: Oxford University Press.
Lave, J., & Wenger, E. (1991). *Situated learning: Legitimate peripheral participation.* Cambridge: Cambridge University Press.
Lawson, H. (2004). The logic of collaboration in education and the human services. *Journal of Interprofessional Care, 18*(3), 225–237.
Leithwood, K. (1992). The move toward transformational leadership. *Educational Leadership, 49*(5), 8–12.
Levin, B. (2006). Schools in challenging circumstances: A reflection on what we know and what we need to know. *School Effectiveness and School Improvement, 17*(4), 399–408.
Lin, N. (1999). Building a network theory of social capital. *Connections, 22*(1), 28–51.
Lincoln, Y., & Guba, E. (1985). *Naturalistic inquiry.* Newbury Park: Sage.
Lindsay, G., Harris, A., Chapman, C., & Muijs, D. (2005). *School federations. Preliminary report to the DfES.* Coventry: University of Warwick.
Ling-Yee, L., & Ogunmonkun, G. O. (2001). The Influence of interfirm relational capabilities on export advantage and performance: An empirical analysis. *International Business Review, 10*, 399–420.
Linn, R. L., Baker, E. L., & Betebenner, D. W. (2002). Accountability systems: Implications of requirements of the no child left behind act of 2001. *Educational Researcher, 31*(6), 3–16.
Lipman, P. (2004). *High stakes education.* London: RoutledgeFalmer.
Luhmann, N. (1997). *Die Gesellschaft der Gesellschaft.* Frankfurt: Suhrkamp.
Martinez, A., Dimitriadis, Y., Rubia, B., Gomez E., & de la Fuente, P. (2003). Combining qualitative evaluation and social network analysis for the study of classroom social interactions. *Computers and Education, 41*(4), 353–368.
McAllister, D. J. (1995). Affect- and cognition-based trust as foundations for interpersonal cooperation in organizations. *Academy of Management Journal 38*(1), 24–59.
McGuire, M., & Agranoff, R. (2007). *Answering the big questions, asking the bigger questions: Expanding the public network management empirical research agenda.* Presented at the Public Management Research Association Conference, Tucson, AZ, October 25–27, 2007.
McMahon, T. J., Ward, N. L., Pruett, M. K., Davidson, L., & Griffith, E. E. H. (2000). Building full-service schools: Lessons learned in the development of interagency collaboratives. *Journal of Educational and Psychological Consultation, 11*(1), 65–92.
Melucci, A. (1980). The new social movements. A theoretical approach. *Theory and Methods, 19*(2), 199–226.
Messiou, K. (2006). Understanding marginalisation in education: The voice of children. *European Journal of Psychology of Education, 21*(3), 305–318.
Miles, M., & Huberman, A. (1994). *Qualitative data analysis.* Thousand Oaks, CA: Sage.

Miles, S., & Kaplan, I. (2005). Using images to promote reflection: An action research study in Zambia and Tanzania. *Journal of Research in Special Educational Needs, 5*(2), 77–83.

Mill, J. S. (1859). *On Liberty*. London: Filliquarian Publishing.

Milward, H. B., & Provan, K. G. (2003, October). *Managing networks effectively.* Paper presented at the national public management research conference, Washington, DC.

Mitra, D. L. (2008). Balancing power in communities of practice: An examination of increasing student voice through school-based youth-adult partnerships. *Journal of Educational Change, 9*(3), 221–242.

Montgomery, D. (2001). Increasing native American Indian involvement in gifted programs in rural schools. *Psychology in the Schools, 38*(5), 467–475.

Muijs, D. (1997). Predictors of academic achievement and academic self-concept: A longitudinal perspective. *British Journal of Educational Psychology, 67*, 263–277.

Muijs, D. (2006a). *Leadership in multi-agency contexts: A case study of extended schools in the UK.* Paper presented at the international congress for school effectiveness and school improvement, Fort Lauderdale, FL, January 2006.

Muijs, D. (2006b). New directions for school effectiveness research: Towards school effectiveness without schools? *Journal of Educational Change, 7*(2), 141–160.

Muijs, D. (2008). Collaboration in a rural school district. *Improving Schools, 11*(1), 61–73.

Muijs, D., Ainscow, M., & West, M. (2007). *Why network? Theoretical perspectives on the value of networking and collaboration.* Paper presented at the annual meeting of the American educational research association, Chicago, IL, April 2007.

Muijs, D., Chapman, C., Armstrong, P., & Collins, A. (2010). *The impact of teach first on leadership and classroom practice: A mixed methods study of the impact of an alternative teacher certification programme on school serving disadvantaged areas.* Paper presented at the international congress for school effectiveness and school improvement, Kuala Lumpur, 3–6 January 2010.

Muijs, D., & Harris, A. (2003). Teacher leadership: Improvement through empowerment? An overview of research. *Educational Management, Administration and Leadership, 31*(4), 437–448.

Muijs, D., & Harris, A. (2007). Teacher leadership in (In)Action: Three case studies of contrasting schools. *Educational, Management, Administration and Leadership, 35*(1), 111–134.

Muijs, D., Harris, A., Chapman, C., Stoll, L., & Russ, J. (2004). Improving schools in socio-economically disadvantaged areas: An overview of research. *School Effectiveness and School Improvement, 15*(2), 149–176.

Muijs, D., & Reynolds, D. (2002). Teacher beliefs and behaviors: What matters. *Journal of Classroom Interaction, 37*(2), 3–15.

Muijs, D., & Reynolds, D. (2010). *Effective teaching, evidence and practice* (3rd ed.). London: Sage.

Munch, R. (2001). History of functionalism. In N. Smelser & B. Baltes (Eds.), *International encyclopedia of the social and behavioral sciences* (pp. 5838–5844). Dordrecht: Elsevier.

Mutz, D. (2002). Cross-cutting social networks: Testing democratic theory in practice. *American Political Science Review, 96*, 111–126.

Nooteboom, B. (2004). *Inter-firm collaboration, networks and strategy: An integrated approach* (1st ed.). New York: Routledge.

Norwich, B., Evans, J., Lunt, I., Steedman, J., & Wedell, K. (1994). Clusters: Inter-school collaboration in meeting special educational needs in ordinary chools. *British Educational Research Journal, 20*(3), 279–291.

Nylen, U. (2007). Interagency collaboration in human services: Impact of formalization and intensity on effectiveness. *Public Administration, 85*(1), 143–166.

O'Neill, O. (2002). *Called to account* (Lecture 3, Reith Lectures 2002). London: BBC. Retrieved from (22/5/2008), http://www.bbc.co.uk/radio4/reith2002/lecture3.shtml

OECD. (2000). *Knowledge management in the learning society.* Paris: OECD.

OECD. (2001). *What schools for the future.* Paris: OECD.

O'Mahoney, S., & Bechky, B. (2008). Boundary organizations: Enabling collaboration among unexpected allies. *Administrative Science Quarterly, 53*(3), 422–459.

Phillips, R., & Harper-Jones, G. (2003). Whatever next? Education policy and New Labour: The first four years, 1997–2001. *British Educational Research Journal, 29*(1), 125–132.

Pinon, D., Samii-Shore, K., & Batchelder, M. (2002). *Principles of learning: 2001–2002 Evaluation report*. Austin, TX: The University of Texas.

Potter, D., Reynolds, D., & Chapman, C. (2002). School improvement for schools facing challenging circumstances: A review of research and practice. *School Leadership and Management, 22*(2), 14–21.

Putnam, R. D. (1995). Bowling alone: America's declining social capital. *Journal of Democracy, 6*(1), 65–78.

Raham, H. (1998). Full service schools. *School Business Affairs, 64*(6), 24–28.

Ravitch, D. (2000). *Left back. A century of battles over school reform*. New York: Simon and Schuster.

Reyes, P., & Phillips, J. C. (2002). *The Houston Annenberg challenge research and evaluation study. Year two evaluation report. Transforming public schools*. Austin, TX: The University of Texas.

Reynolds, D. (2007). *Schools learning from their best. The within school variation (WSV) project*. Nottingham: National College for School Leadership.

Riley, K., & Jordan, J. (2004). "It makes sense to me": Reforming classrooms from the bottom up: a case study in change. *Improving Schools, 7*(3), 227–242.

Ritter, T., Wilkinson, I., & Johnston, W. (2003). Managing in complex business networks. *Industrial Marketing Management, 33*(3), 175–183.

Sailor, W. (2002). *Whole-school success and inclusive education*. New York: Teachers College Press.

Sanders, M. G. (1999). Schools' programs and progress in the national network of partnership schools. *Journal of Educational Research, 92*(4), 220–229.

Schein, E. H. (2001). Clinical inquiry/research. In P. Reason & H. Bradbury (Eds.), *Handbook of action research* (pp. 266–279). London: Sage.

Schon, D. (1991). *The reflective practitioner* (2nd ed.). San Francisco: Jossey Bass.

Schwandt, T. A., & Halpern, E. S. (1988). *Linking auditing and metaevaluation: Enhancing quality in applied research*. London: Sage.

Segre, S. (2004). A Durkheimian network theory. *Journal of Classical Sociology, 4*(2), 215–235.

Senge, P. M. (1990). *The fifth discipline: The art and practice of the learning organization*. New York: Doubleday/Currency.

Senge, P., Cambron-McCabe, N., Lucas, B., Smith, T., Dutton, J., & Kleiner, A. (2000). *Schools that learn: A fifth discipline fieldbook for educators, parents, and everyone who cares about education*. New York: Doubleday.

Sergiovanni, T. (1999). The story of community. In J. Retallick, B. Cocklin, & K. Coombe (Eds.), *Learning communities in education: Issues, strategies and contexts* (pp. 9–25). London: Routledge.

Simmel, G. (1950). In K. Wolff (Ed. & trans.), *The sociology of Georg Simmel*. Glencoe, IL: The Free Press.

Social Exclusion Unit. (2001). *Preventing social exclusion*. London: Social Exclusion Unit.

Statham, J. (2004). Effective services to support children in special circumstances. *Child Care, Health and Development, 30*, 589–598.

Stoll, L. (1999). Realising our potential: Understanding and developing capacity for lasting improvement. *School Effectiveness and Improvement, 10*(4), 503–532.

Stoll, L., Fink, D., & Earl, L. (2003). *It's about learning; And it's about time*. London: Routledge Falmer.

Sullivan, H., & Skelcher, C. (2002). *Collaborating across boundaries*. London: Palgrave.

Sze, S. (2004). *Barriers to school success for students with disabilities in rural communities*. Niagara Falls, NY: Niagara University.

Teddlie, C., & Reynolds, D. (Eds.). (2000). *International handbook of school effectiveness research.* London: Falmer Press.

Thurlow, M., Vandercook, T., McDevitt, M., Medwetz, L., Nelson, M., Sauer, J., & Walz, L. (1999). *District partnership approach to inclusion: A qualitative evaluation of impact.* Minneapolis, MN: Institute on Community Integration, University of Minnesota.

Tichy, N., Tushman, M., & Fombrun, C. (1979). Social network analysis for organizations. *Academy of Management Review, 4*(4), 507–519.

Uzzi, B. (1996). The sources and consequences of embeddedness for the economic performance of organisations: The network effect. *American Sociological Review, 61*, 674–698.

Valente, T. (1996). Social network thresholds in the diffusion of information. *Social Networks, 18*, 69–89.

Van Veen, D., Day, C., & Walraven, G. (Eds.). (1998). *Multi-service schools: Integrated services for children and youth at risk.* Leuven/Apeldoom: Garant.

Vygotsky, L., Vygotsky, S., & John-Steiner, V. (Eds.). (1978). *Mind in society: The development of higher psychological processes.* Cambridge, MA: Harvard University Press.

Wallace, M. (1998). A counter-policy to subvert education reform? Collaboration among schools and colleges in a competitive climate. *British Educational Research Journal, 24*(2), 195–215.

Walter, A., Ritter, T., & Gemunde, H. G. (2001). Value creation in buyer–seller relationships: Theoretical considerations and empirical results from a supplier's perspective. *Industrial Marketing Management, 30*(4), 365–377.

Warmington, P. (2004). *New wine into old skins: Rethinking professional learning for emerging "Joined Up" practice in the UK.* Paper presented at the professional learning in a changing society conference, Oslo.

Weick, K. (1995). *Sensemaking in organizations.* Thousand Oaks, CA: Sage Publications.

Wenger, E. (1998). *Communities of practice: Learning, meaning and identity* Cambridge: Cambridge University Press.

West, A. (2008). Redistribution and financing schools in England under labour: Are resources going to where needs are greatest? *Education Management Administration and Leadership, 37*(2), 158–179.

West, M., Ainscow, M., & Muijs, D. (2006). *Collaboration for school improvement. A report for the national college for school leadership.* Manchester: University of Manchester.

West, M., Ainscow, M., & Stanford, J. (2005). Sustaining improvement in schools in challenging circumstances: A study of successful practice. *School Leadership and Management, 25*(1): 77–93.

West, M., & Muijs, D. (2006). *Improving schools in complex and challenging circumstances through school-to school collaboration: A review of key findings from recent UK initiatives promoting school partnership arrangements.* Paper presented at the European conference on educational research, Geneva, Switzerland, September 2006.

Author Index

Subject Index

The manufacturer's authorised representative in the EU is Springer Nature Customer Service Centre GmbH, Europaplatz 3, 69115 Heidelberg, Germany. If you have any concerns regarding our products, please contact ProductSafety@springernature.com

Printed and bound by CPI Group (UK) Ltd, Croydon, CR0 4YY
25/09/2026
02222869-0002